Value Investing in Growth Companies

Value Investing in Growth Companies

HOW TO SPOT HIGH GROWTH BUSINESSES AND GENERATE 40% TO 400% INVESTMENT RETURNS

Rusmin Ang and Victor Chng

WILEY

Other Wiley Editorial Offices
John Wiley & Sons, 111 River Street, Hoboken, NJ 07030, USA
John Wiley & Sons, The Atrium, Southern Gate, Chichester, West Sussex, PO19
    8SQ, United Kingdom
John Wiley & Sons (Canada) Ltd., 5353 Dundas Street West, Suite 400, Toronto,
    Ontario, M9B 6HB, Canada
John Wiley & Sons Australia Ltd., 42 McDougall Street, Milton, Queensland 4064,
    Australia
Wiley-VCH, Boschstrasse 12, D-69469 Weinheim, Germany

ISBN 978–1–118–56779–1 (Cloth)
ISBN 978–1–118–56795–1 (ePDF)
ISBN 978–1–118–56797–5 (Mobi)
ISBN 978–1–118–56798–2 (ePub)

Typeset in 11/13 pt. ITC New Baskerville by MPS Limited, Chennai, India.
Printed in Singapore by Ho Printing Singapore Pte Ltd

10 9 8 7 6 5 4 3 2 1

Contents

x   Contents

Foreword

After reading this book, you might come away with the feeling that Victor and Rusmin have seriously pounded Singapore's pavements in search of value-growth companies. Not only have they traveled East Coast Parkway to Changi Village and back to the central business district (scouring for value companies) in Singapore, but they have also been out to Woodlands to check out its industrial zone. Bottom-up investing is all about discovering a company's value early, getting its stocks well before the crowds, and exiting (hopefully with a profit) as mainstream investors move in and push up the valuation. Typically, these sorts of opportunities are found within second- and third-line stocks rather than well-known blue chips. It is a long-term strategy that requires discipline and patience, on top of a robust system, to have a reasonable chance of success.

Despite their differing backgrounds, Victor and Rusmin have merged paths, and value investing has become their common identity. In my opinion, it takes guts to write a book in the first place, but talent to write about a process that has merit and can be empirically tested over time to add value.

This book provides for an entertaining read that takes you through a system that, if followed closely, should help you identify quality stocks and reject unfavorable ones. There is, of course, no guarantee that following this system is a sure recipe for instant riches. However, it certainly provides a comprehensive check that would help you avoid investing in dud stocks and steer you toward those with solid fundamentals and decent rerating potential over time.

After reading this book, it will serve as a ready-to-use reference. The techniques outlined herein are timeless and can be referred to over and over again as you make progress in your investment journey. This is an enlightening read, and thoroughly enjoyable for those interested in learning about value-growth investing and start-ing their investing journey.

Digby Falkiner
Former Indonesian Research Director at Deutsche Bank
Former Regional Research Operations Head at
Societe Generale Private Investor and
Lead Trainer for Millionaire Investor Program Advanced

Preface

Value investing has been one of the most consistent and proven methods of generating wealth over the last century (or more). The third-richest man in the world, Warren Buffett, who has made value investing his lifetime passion, is worth $46 billion. You don't have to be like Buffett, managing billions in the spotlight; a lot of ordinary people with ordinary jobs are perfectly happy quietly making millions through value investing. They are your quintessential millionaires next door.

It makes sense. Spend less than you earn, save diligently, and, when the opportunity comes around, invest cheaply in great companies that will grow in value many, many times over the long run. It's a safe, logical formula to long-term financial security and success. You don't have to be a superstar athlete, movie actor, or tech guru to be financially free. Anyone with a normal job and the diligent application of value investing can retire with millions.

While value investing is traditionally associated with investing in well-established companies, in this book, we'll show you how you can further increase your investment returns by value investing in smaller growth companies. Investing in growth companies does give us some lucrative compounding rates, but it also requires us to possess the appropriate knowledge to invest in these companies, as these investments can be risky. This book is meant to help you achieve the same success that we have had with growth companies. In doing so, we would like to impart a step-by-step process as to how to value these companies with little risk and still be able to generate 15 percent compounded returns annually.

We know you picked up this book because you want to learn more about investing in growth companies. Whether you are a seasoned investor or a newbie who wants to learn about value investing in growth companies, this book is for you.

With a growing global population, increased life expectancy, rising standards of living, and affluence, more and more will be spent on consuming new products and services, therein fueling the world's economy every year. However, the economy is subject to fluctuations—the booms and busts of economic cycles are inevitable—but new millionaires are created virtually every cycle. There is no better time than right now to get yourself on the road to riches by buying something that is going to be worth more money 10 years from now.

Let us share with you a brutal fact—if you place your money in a bank, you will be earning interest that is lower than the average inflation rate in most countries, be it in Indonesia, Malaysia, Singapore, China, or Thailand, where you will effectively lose value on your money. Instead of doing that, an alternative is to invest your money and allow it to compound over the long haul.

All investors have a common aspiration to enjoy a good return on their investment. But how do we identify investment strategies that can consistently beat the market? One of the greatest things about investing is that there are numerous strategies that investors can deploy, ranging from technical charting to fundamentals analysis. Different techniques produce different sets of results, each with different risk levels. When there are profits to be made, there are risks involved. It is highly dependent on the investor to choose the right strategies that yield the most consistent returns with the lowest risks and yet be able to outperform the market in the long run.

Rusmin Ang's Journey

Like many of you, I dreamed of becoming financially free. When I was just eight years old, I promised my parents that I would make big bucks and buy them big toys, like bungalows and sports cars, some day. Seeing how ambitious I was at a young age, my parents were delighted, but took my promise with a pinch of salt.

Soon after I graduated from secondary school in Indonesia, my sister and my mum decided to send me to Singapore to further my education. Arriving in Singapore at the age of 15, I felt very foreign, as I could not read, write, or speak English or Mandarin. That did not stop me from studying hard to better cope with the education system in Singapore.

Over the years, I occasionally have flashbacks about the promise I made to my parents. Driven by a desire to become financially free, I decided to take action and began to learn how to grow my wealth in order to fulfill my promise to them. I read *Rich Dad Poor Dad* and *Rich Dad's Cashflow Quadrant* by Robert Kiyosaki, books I strongly recommend to those who want to transform their lives. Through these books, I learned the mindset of successful people and identified my cash-flow quadrant, a conceptual tool used in those books.

From then on, my life changed, and I started to seek active ways to become financially free. In my bid to learn more about investments, I attended preview seminars for trading, such as options trading and foreign exchange trading (FOREX). Very often, these programs appeared very promising, as they seemed to be offering a way by which to become rich within a short time. But, as I was a student who did not have much money, I never enrolled in the courses. Looking back, I am glad I did not.

I realized that the only way for me to learn about investment was through traditional methods. So, I went to the library to read about candlesticks, a method that was developed by the Japanese for those who wanted to become experts in trading. However, I could not comprehend how one could predict the future (e.g., market movements) just by looking at technical charts that are based on historical prices and volumes. Also, it was too daunting to have to memorize all the terms used in the candlestick chart in order to arrive at a decision as to whether a sign is favorable or not.

Soon after, I discovered that legendary investor Warren Buffett was once a trader who tried to master so-called technical analysis, a technique which he later found to be worthless, and that had cost him about eight years trying to master it.

Inspired by his story, I decided to give up what little trading technique I had acquired and directed my focus toward value investing. Abiding by the saying "If you want to be the best, you've got to learn from the best," I began to read all the books I could find about Warren Buffett's strategies. Initially, I went through a slow learning process with no tangible returns on my investments. However, I started to learn much more when I took action and attended Millionaire Investor Program (MIP), a course conducted by Ken Chee and Clive Tan during August 2009.

Victor Chng's Journey

Financial news of a reported Singapore Straits Time Index (STI) crash—from its peak of 3,241 points in 2008 to its lowest level of 1,456 points in March 2009—caused the value of almost every stock price to dip as never before. The financial crisis of 2008–09, caused mainly by U.S. subprime mortgages, impacted many investors, but fortunately, not me. With the onset of a financial crisis, I had a gut feeling that it was the perfect time to invest, because I, like many others, abide by the investment philosophy of buying low and selling high.

At one point, I was glued to the screen of my laptop every single day, with hopes to catch the bottom of the Singapore Exchange Traded Fund (ETF) Index cycle before it recovered. Then my instincts were telling me to invest all my money in it. However, I was confronted with a fear that prices would continue to fall after buying into the fund. My emotions ran wild and I was more confused when the index plunged further. I knew I did not possess the knowledge to evaluate the stocks, and thus had no choice but to stay out of the market.

One day, it suddenly dawned on me that I was once told that the third-richest man on the planet earned his fortune purely by investing. Intrigued by how this man landed his fortune, I did my research and learned that the person was Warren Buffett. Widely regarded as one of the most successful investors in the world, Warren Buffett, as I had gathered, used the investment technique commonly known as *value investing*.

By November 2008, I was reading books about value investing and doing my best to understand value-investing concepts. However, I knew that I needed a mentor who could impart the right skills to me in order for me to shorten my learning curve. With that intention, I started browsing newspapers and the Internet, with hopes of finding a mentor. There was very little to be learned about value investing, as most investors were vested in trading.

In my heart, I knew that the wealthiest people (a very small, elite group) are rich because they do things differently from everybody else. In my heart, I knew that I had to do things differently to reap extraordinary results.

With this belief, I steered my investments away from the vast majority of investors out there who were traders, while I continued my search for a befitting mentor to guide me on my investment journey.

In March 2009, I was reading the newspaper when the term *value investing* in an advertisement caught my eye. Without hesitation, I made an inquiry about the advertisement and booked my seat for a preview session. After the preview, I was convinced that the course was what I had always been searching for, and decided to sign up for it. Called the Millionaire Investor Program (MIP), a course taught by Ken Chee and Clive Tan.

How We Met

The power of MIP was what brought us together. After the course, we embarked on our respective investment journeys. What was good about the program was that it allowed us to have unlimited reviews. As a result, we volunteered to be logistics helpers to add more value to new participants, while we continued to build our own knowledge of value investing. We met each other when we were part of the logistics team and realized that we have the same philosophy of investing in fast-growing companies (or growth companies that grow at more than 15 percent per year in terms of revenue and net profit).

With this common interest, we formed a mastermind group that mostly focuses on unraveling growth companies. Conducted monthly, our masterminding group provides us with a platform to unearth high-potential growth companies listed in Singapore Exchange Limited (SGX) and place them on our investment radar. At this pace, our investment momentum is kept going, while we provide each other mutual support throughout our investment journey. We also get to conduct *scuttle-butting* (a term used by Philip Fisher in reference to carrying out investigations on the ground) as a team, a concept that will be explored in a later chapter.

For now, let us just say that we used scuttle-butting in January 2010 to unearth the potential of a company called Design Studio Furniture Limited, an interior design company that grew at a compound rate of more than 30 percent per year in revenue and net profits from 2005 to 2009. We realized that its fundamentals were quite sound and that it consistently generated high free cash flow for the previous five years. However, we were concerned about its valuation, as it was overpriced, and there was not enough margin of safety at $0.66. We decided to place this company on our radar.

Our patience was soon well rewarded. On May 2010, Design Studio announced that they were in a lawsuit with a Dubai company for alleged breach of contractual obligations. Mr. Market (a famous metaphor created by the father of value investing, Benjamin Graham) had a huge mood swing and slapped the company hard; its stock price plunged from $0.60 to $0.45 within a month! Upon learning about this, we immediately revalued the company and found that we had a margin of safety of 50 percent, based on the assumption of 0 percent growth rates.

We made an appointment with the management to learn more about the lawsuit and found, at the end of it, that the lawsuit did not have any impact on its business. We concluded that the business appeared to be in a temporary crisis, not a long-term entanglement. As a result, we started purchasing Design Studio at $0.45. Within two months, it rose to $0.64, increasing by more than 40 percent from our purchase price.

While we were writing this book, Design Studio announced that they had won the litigation case. Although that was the first stock we had bought since the inception of our mastermind group, it was not beginners' luck that we had nailed a good investment. Instead, it had to do with what we had learned from the program. As long-term investors, we have learned that time is in our favor and that patience is what is needed to become successful investors.

Thereafter, a food and beverages (F&B) company we uncovered was Japan Food Holding Limited, a Japanese restaurant with compound growth at above 20 percent per year in revenue and net profits from 2006 to 2010. Its fundamentals were sound; we even visited their point of sales in Indonesia. To our surprise, their franchise outlets in Jakarta, Indonesia, were doing extremely well, even during nonpeak periods. In Singapore, most of their outlets were doing pretty well when we visited them. In August 2011 we started purchasing their stock at $0.25. In seven months, the price of the stock advanced to $0.43, and our investment grew by 72 percent. A telling sign that the business is a good investment—even though it has yet to report its profits in its upcoming financial statement— is that its restaurants are constantly filled with customers. What is more convincing is that Japan Food reported growth in earnings even during the financial crisis, proving to be a recession-proof business that is little known to financial analysts and financial institutions.

Owing to investment performances that reaped real results, we were promoted to coaches. Today, we coach fresh graduates and guide them as to how to conduct their own mastermind groups. As a coach, we teach them how to apply the knowledge that they have gained during the program. In doing so, we acquire new insights from other investors as well. In the course of coaching others, we find it extremely enriching to network with people from different industries. At the same time, we learn of more undervalued stocks that become opportunities for future investments. As we learned over time, being a coach is not about teaching, but about networking—increasing our circles of competence and sharpening our investment knowledge.

Overview of the Contents

In chapter 1, we will discuss how an average investor starts their investment journey. We will introduce the concepts of pure value investing and pure growth investing. By combining the pros of each technique, we eliminate the cons and thereby create a concept that, in fact, has been around for decades. We will refer to this technique as the *value-growth investing strategy*. Here, an investment strategy, also known as an *investment style*, is defined as an approach to choose good investments that produce excellent returns.

Used by successful investors such as Warren Buffett and Peter Lynch, value-growth investing has produced real results with consistent compounded returns of more than 20 percent every year. Since their methods are proven, we, as retail investors, can adopt them in Asia's emerging market to generate *multi-baggers* (a term used by Peter Lynch) in return. In layman's terms, this translates to investing $200 in a particular company and having its value grow to $1,000. In this case, Peter Lynch will call it a *five-bagger*, or five times your initial return ($1,000/$200 = 5). Here, we will shed light on what exactly are growth companies and how value-growth investors make money from them.

Before we unveil the proven technique as to how to buy growth companies at bargain prices, you must first understand the mindset of a successful investor. By that, we mean the habits that you need to develop, master, and instill in your life—habits which we will be sharing in chapter 2—before you are ready to embark on the journey toward joining the millionaire's club.

In chapter 3, we will be revealing a simple model to successful investing. This model will be further explored in chapters 4, 5, 6, and 7. In chapter 8, we will be focusing on how you can use this model to help you make a decision on whether to buy, monitor, or sell a stock. We will also guide you as to how you can screen a stock that could potentially become the next multi-bagger.

Along the way, investors must have a good knowledge as to how to manage growth companies in their portfolios. We cover this in chapter 9.

However, mistakes are inevitable when it comes to investing, and our goal is to commit fewer mistakes and uncover more bargain gems. By doing so, we can effectively maximize our returns and minimize our risks. So, in chapter 10, you will learn about common mistakes made by investors and how you can avoid making these mistakes. Last, as a bonus chapter, we will showcase five companies as case studies and will demonstrate how we apply the model, from the perspective of value-growth investors. For this, you will need to download the case studies from www .MillionaireInvestor.com/5-case-studies.

Acknowledgments

From Rusmin Ang

When Ken Chee first approached us, I found it daunting for two young chaps to write a book. Nevertheless, Victor and I took it as a challenge and embarked on writing this book with deep regard for our readers.

To Ken Chee and Clive Tan, thank you for your full support and for unearthing a talent that was unbeknownst to me. You are indeed my business partners, mentors, friends, and family.

To my partner, Victor Chng, this book would not have been possible without your effort, commitment, and encouragement. If not for your Muay Thai buddies (Tommy Ng, Ding Jun He, Bruce Dierl, and Paul Chen), we would not have had the finesse to write this book through the many nights and long weekends during the span of six months, given the fact that both of us hold full-time jobs!

To the many successful investors who serve as a source of inspiration—Warren Buffett, John Burr William, Charlie Munger, Philip Fisher, Benjamin Graham, Peter Lynch, Jim Collins, Peter Lim, Li Ka Shing, Robert Kiyosaki, as well as other successful investors—you have unknowingly made me a better investor with your wisdom, timeless principles, and philosophies. Thank you!

To 8 Investment Team and Partners—Ken Chee, Clive Tan, Victor Chng, Ivan Ho, Cynthia Seen, Lori Chin, Phyllis Chan, Pauline Teo, Murphy Ong, Linghui Ong, Adam Wong, Kenji Tay, Heah Min An, Jenny Loo, Attlee Hue, and Digby Falkiner—all of you are truly masters in your own areas. Without the MIP Program, I would not have had the chance to know all of you. Thank you for not only offering insightful feedback on this book, but also for all your love and support. So any imperfections found in this book the responsibility of the authors, not their lack of effort. Inarguably, they deserve praise for making this book possible.

To the team at Wiley—Nick Wallwork, Gemma Rosey Diaz, Stefan Skeen, and Jules Yap—thank you for making this book international. You guys deserve the credit!

To my family, you might not have known that I was writing this book, but I am deeply grateful to all of you nonetheless. Thank you for showering me with freedom and love, as well as respect for the decisions that I make in my life. Without your influence, I would not be who I am today. I am truly very blessed to be have been born into this family.

To my ex-colleagues, polytechnic, and O-level mates, thank you for our long-standing friendships. You guys are indeed awesome! Last, to the many others whom I have left out of this book, thank you for being a part of my life and for having enriched my life in one way or another.

From Victor Chng

My original idea was to write a simple set of notes for our internal network of investors to further advance their investing education. However, when I bounced this idea off my mentor, Ken, he told me to write a full book instead, to reach out to more people who could benefit from this financial and investing knowledge.

That really caught me by surprise but, eventually, Rusmin and I decided to take on the seemingly daunting challenge. All of this would not have been possible if not for all the wonderful people who have had such a positive impact on my life.

To my investment mentors, Ken Chee and Clive Tan, thank you for introducing the world of value investing to me. You transformed a spendthrift with zero financial knowledge into someone who now not only knows the true value of money but also how to invest and build lifetime wealth. I deeply appreciate the trust you have in me in managing the private fund with you at 8 Investment.

To my fellow investment analyst Rusmin. This book is possible only because you agreed to write it with me. Thank you for your effort and the commitment you put into this book. The generosity you show in always sharing your investing knowledge with me is something I truly appreciate. You are a great friend.

To my 8 Investment team and our partners: Pauline Teo, Adam Wong, Kenji Tay, Heah Min An, Murphy Ong, Phyllis Chan, Cynthia Seen, Jenny Loo, Ivan Ho, Atlee Hue, Digby Falkiner, Lori Chin, and Linghui Ong. Thank you for making our workplace so fun and enjoyable. You all make the Millionaire Investor Program experience what it is today; thank you for always sharing your knowledge with me in the areas that you are expert in. You guys are awesome!

To the mentors who have had an impact on me through your books, the things you do, or if I had the pleasure to work with you: Warren Buffett, Charlie Munger, Peter Lynch, Anthony Bolton, Stephen Convey, Stuart Tan, Adam Khoo, John Neff, Robert Kiyosaki, Kerry Zurier, Marshall Thurber, Bill Allen, and Eric Feng. Thank you! You have had an impact on my life.

To my family members: Jeff Chng, Wendy Tan, Vince Chng, Valerie Chng, and Vance Chng. Thank you for all your support.

To my girlfriend, Constance Quek. Thank you for being my listening ear and always being there to support me in everything I do. I want to tell you I truly appreciate all that you've done, and that I am blessed to have you by my side.

To my Hilltop Muay Thai brothers: Tommy Ng, Ding Junhe, Ding Jun Cheng, Paul Chen, Tan Shao Wen, Bruce Dierl, Peter Yeo, and Jay, Mic, and Andy Lai. We have been through many tough journeys in life, and yet we always charge forward because we never give up. Thank you guys for always being there to support me in life, and in Muay Thai training!

To my polytechnic friends: Satyish Kumar, Wan Jun Jie, Chua Jie Wei, Salleh, Jeremy Singh, Zita Mok, Ong Chun Mei, Ng Jia Lin, Ng Jianwen, Desmond Chua, and Fu Shan Wei. Thank you for making polytechnic life so incredibly fun.

To my army friends: Jasper Nai, Edwin Ngoh, Alvin Tan, Geh Si yuan, William Hu, Luke Vijay, Teo Wei Hong, Tan Toh Jin, Xu Bao Feng, Kenny Ng, Brendan Wong, Benjiamin Chen, Xiong Qiang, Pek Chee Lim, Chua Liang Sheng, Boon Jun Yan, Daniel Mak, Lim You Lok, Gladwin Chen, Nicholas Lim, and William Yeung. Thank you for making an impact on my life. I learned a lot of things from you guys (good and bad!) during my army days.

Special thanks to everyone at John Wiley & Sons, TLC Friends, Millionaire Investor Program, Brand Mastery, Money and You, 8 Investment, JM Asia, and Future of Business, as well as others whom I may have left out. You guys make a difference in the world around you.

CHAPTER 1

The Making
of a Value-Growth Investor

The Common Journey of New Investors

In this era of investing, new investors are born every day. This new generation of investors, typically young adults, are intrigued by the idea of investing and enticed by the ups and downs of the stock market. Such is their interest in investing, so many enter the stock market without knowing much about it, with the hopes of achieving their dreams within the shortest period of time. Lured by the temptation to make quick profits, many young or inexperienced investors rush into the stock market without adequate knowledge.

There are those who, upon hearing how their friends got burned in the stock market, either promise themselves to stay away or caution themselves to learn more about investing before entering into a highly volatile market. After all, prevention is always better than cure. To them, it is senseless to gamble away hard-earned money that can be put to other money-generating uses.

In the world of investments, those who are not knowledgeable or have the wrong perception about investing can be classified as beginners or novice investors. Among these novice investors, we may classify them into two categories of investors: risk-averse investors and risk-taker investors.

Risk-averse investors are conservative investors who constantly look for ways to minimize investment risks as much as possible. By attending courses and seminars and reading books, they hope to acquire investment knowledge before placing their money into the stock market. On the other hand, risk-taker investors are those who lack the knowledge to invest on their own but rely solely on the advice of sources (e.g., hot tips, rumors) to make investment decisions. As they trust professionals or those who appear to have more expertise than they do, this category of investors values the opinion of stock brokers, friends, or even relatives when it comes to investing.

Although risk-averse investors take the necessary precautions to prevent themselves from losing money in the stock market simply by choosing to first acquire investment knowledge, many of them fail to acquire appropriate investment knowledge. More often than not, they end up attending investment courses that promise to earn them a quick profit within a short period of time. On the other hand, risk-taker investors are less patient (short term) and lack the emotional detachment necessary for effective investing. They try to take shortcuts by relying on investment tips and learn from their mistakes only when they incur debt or lose a huge sum of money. To this group of investors, the stock market is just another gambling venue in which to place their bets. As a result, these two categories of investors often end up as short-term traders.

Highly speculative by nature, short-term trading leverages short-term market fluctuations to make a profit within a period of less than a month. In short-term trading, common technical charting tools are based on price are moving averages, Japanese candlestick patterns, Gantt charts, and resistance levels. These tools are used to help traders make decisions on when to buy and sell. Short-term traders know that it is all about being at the right place at the right time in order to make money. In fact, some traders would not hesitate to leverage to get more returns upon hearing a hot tip that a trading pattern is in favor.

Short-Term Trading to Long-Term Investing

While we are happy for this group of traders if such methods work for them, we must acknowledge that a short-term trader takes more risks. And, even if the technique works beautifully, would you want to spend most of your time monitoring fluctuations of a particular stock in order to make a profit? Obviously not! Life is more than just making money in the stock market. We want our source of income to be as passive as possible, so that money flows in continuously, and we can spend the rest of time with our loved ones. Do not let the stock market own you!

Moreover, short-term trading can also be unsuitable for those who do not have adequate time, financial resources, and education—attributes that are often less accessible to individual traders as opposed to big institutional players.

The media tends to give a lot of attention to how traders make money within a short period of time but often forget to mention how other traders lose money too. Many forget the phrase *slow and steady wins the race.*

> *When it comes to investing, many forget the phrase* slow and steady wins the race.

Many investors confess their regrets regarding entering the stock market as short-term investors only after having burned their fingers. Having spoken to many investors, we know of friends who have decided to become long-term investors as a result. They shift their focus from monitoring the price and volume of transactions to comprehending the basic fundamentals of businesses, such as company earnings. Doing so makes the whole investment process easier and more logical.

It's not so much which strategy works best for you but the kind of lifestyle you want: freedom and choice to do what you want without having to worry about money. If that's your

> *The main setback for investors who fail to become successful is spending too much time looking at stock prices.*

goal, then long-term investment will suit you best and take care of your wealth. Sad to say, however, you can't drive a car by looking at its rearview mirror. Though that's important, what is ultimately more important is what's coming on your way. That's the factor we need to take care and spend most of time looking at. Genius is not required to understand this simple concept. The main setback for investors who fail to become successful is spending too much time looking at historical prices of a stock. As a long-term successful investor, you will need to pay close attention to factors such as whether a core business will still be relevant 10, 20, or 30 years from now, a factor that will affect its future value.

That makes up the majority of content in this book. If applied extensively to growth companies, the ideas presented here might positively widen your investment knowledge and raise the percentage of compounded returns on your current investment portfolio.

While traders pay attention to price and volume, long-term investors look at value. These are value investors and growth investors. No matter what kind of investor they are, everyone starts with zero knowledge in investing. This includes the world's richest investor, Warren Buffett, as well as successful investors in Asia, like Peter Lim, Li Ka Shing, Teng Ngiek Lian, Tan Teng Boo, and Cheah Cheng Hye, who receive tremendous returns on their investments because they look at factors that could affect the future value of companies. Now let us briefly discuss these two categories.

Growth Investors

Fast-growing companies and industries are where growth investors channel their investment focus. They are bullish about a company's future because of promising products, services, or industries. They believe that its value will increase over time as earnings increase, which will eventually catch up with the current trading price. For that reason, growth investors are willing to pay a premium price (e.g., higher price-to-earnings [PE] ratio) in anticipation that a company will deliver higher earnings growth moving forward.

One of the core objectives is to find the key growth driver(s) in a company. Fundamentally, growth investors believe the main growth driver of a stock's share price is earnings growth. It could be derived from management's vision or the promise of an industry that a business is in, which would drive up earnings per share in the future. For instance, in 2010, the management of listed firm Q&M Dental Group announced its intention to increase its number of clinics from 40 to 60 in Singapore and to add 50 new clinics in China by 2015. As a result of the company's vision, many investors came forward and pushed its price above its normal trading price to a PE ratio of more than 50! It goes to show that growth investors look to invest in companies with quality management teams that deliver sales growth, stable margins, and higher earnings growth, demonstrated in a three- to five-year track record.

> Visit five companies in an industry, ask intelligent questions about the points of strength and weaknesses of the other four competitors, and nine times out of ten, a surprisingly detailed and accurate picture of all five will emerge.
>
> —*Philip Fisher*

There are other techniques that growth investors use to assess the key growth drivers of a company, and one such technique is commonly known as *scuttle butting*. This approach to investing was pioneered by Philip Fisher in his book *Common Stocks and Uncommon Profits*. In it, he wrote, "Visit five companies in an industry, ask them intelligent questions about the points of strength and weaknesses of the other four competitors, and nine times out of ten, a surprisingly detailed and accurate picture of all five will emerge." Fisher also suggests that useful information can be obtained from vendors, customers, research scientists, and executives of trade associations. Fisher's strategy is commonly known as the *qualitative approach* (focusing on the quality side of a stock, as opposed to quantitative side, which deals with numbers). In other words, before buying a stock, Fisher will evaluate product and service quality, management ability, future possibilities for growth, and the power of competitors that might bring the company down. These are key assessments when deciding whether a company is a good-quality growth company.

It is very rewarding for the growth investor if the future growth of the company continues to rise. But there is a catch. Downside risks also tend to be higher for growth investors, as they tend to purchase stocks without a sufficient margin of safety. They often overpay because so many investors are eager to invest in a high potential growth company (although the growth may not be realized yet), and growth investors have high expectations that these stocks will outperform the market. They expect a company's growth revenue, earnings, and prices to go up, especially those companies in a hot industry or have glamour stocks that are growing at more than 50 percent annually. However, when these hot stocks miss their earnings prediction, investment returns are greatly affected. This is called a *growth trap*.

The growth investing approach is also known as a *qualitative approach*. It means looking at a business and its management alone, without much consideration for quantitative factors like valuation. Since future prospects are not reflected in financial statements, paying a premium price is still considered rational.

Value Investors

Value investors seek to buy companies that are trading at bargain prices. In other words, they look for a stock that is trading at a bargain price of $0.50, for example, when its business value is $1. They look for companies with low debt and high return on equity, while purchasing them at a great discount. Value investors take on lesser risks than growth investors, as the price they pay is far lower than that paid by growth investors, which explains why value investing continues to outperform the overall market. Value investors wait patiently for the market to realize the value of a company over time and sell only when the market price of the stock is close to or above its intrinsic valuation. It often occurs when the market starts to appreciate the company's true value over time.

This approach to investing was pioneered by Benjamin Graham in his book *The Intelligent Investor.* As an investor, Graham looks out for undervalued companies with sound fundamentals with stock prices that are temporarily beaten down. He is famous for developing the concept of *margin of safety* (the percentage of difference between purchase price and intrinsic value), intrinsic value, and Mr. Market.[1] If Mr. Market's price is unreasonably high, then investors have the opportunity to sell. If it is unreasonably low, then investors have the opportunity to buy.

Value investors tend to focus much more on capital preservation than on stocks that can appreciate in value. In other words, they look to purchase bargain stocks with a greater margin of safety. This serves as a buffer when errors are made in an investment decision and significantly reduces the risks of the investment because the downside is limited. However, some bargains might turn out to be problematic, even when the numbers are healthy and seemingly attractive enough to be bought. This is one of the common mistakes made by value investors who fall into a value trap. Such a value trap is prevalent in stocks that are unloved and unwanted. The fundamentals of such undervalued companies start to deteriorate because there are no growth drivers present.

Value investing in its original and pure form is quantitative in approach. This means looking at numbers and valuation alone, to

---

[1] *Mr. Market* refers to the general stock market. The term was coined by Benjamin Graham.

the exclusion of qualitative factors, such as the quality of the business and its management. However, over time, value investing has evolved into a more advanced technique in which it combines qualitative elements in the strategy. So, for now, we shall focus on differentiating the two techniques, so that we can compare the pros and cons of each one.

Value Investors versus Growth Investors

We created Table 1.1 to help you better understand the differences between the two investing approaches.

A pure value investor tends to ignore the business and its management. As long as the ratios are favorable and the stock is trading at a bargain price—cheap valuation—it is a good sign for them. When there is no growth, the company's fundamentals can only go sideways or down. This method is purely quantitative.

On the other hand, growth investors spend most of their time assessing the quality of the business and its management by using techniques like scuttle butting to filter outstanding companies from mediocre ones. Historical numbers are not a major concern. To them, paying a premium price for a quality and outstanding company is reasonable when its future earnings are believed to be able to catch up with the high price. The returns will still be positive if things (e.g., expansion plans) turn out as planned. In this case, their strategy is purely qualitative. When future revenue and earnings turn out to be below their expectations, share prices will also have fallen, which leads to a growth trap; the company is unable to produce continuous good growth results, as originally planned. The drop in share price translates into immediate loss for the

Table 1.1   Value investors versus growth investors

	Pure Value Investors	Pure Growth investors
Business	No	Yes
Management	No	Yes
Numbers	Yes	No
Valuation	Yes	No
Method	Quantitative	Qualitative
Mistakes	Value trap	Growth trap

investors, since the price paid for the share was at a premium and there was no allowance made for errors. The amount was paid in advance for anticipated high results that did not materialize and may never happen in future. Compared to value investors who insist on a margin of safety, growth investors suffer higher risks of losing money but higher potential to make fat capital appreciation if growth stories pan out.

From another perspective, you can better determine the main focus of each style of investing and the amount of time needed to produce a good return using a time horizon that comprises past, present, and future.

Figure 1.1 shows that growth investors spend more time looking at future drivers of growth in a quality company in the present time. Growth investors focus mainly on factors that would increase future earnings. For instance, companies in a promising industry, such as the energy and technology industries, would be growth investors' targets for the rest of the twenty-first century. In addition, companies that have a promising expansion plan tend to get higher valuations over a company that is out of the limelight. The companies with higher valuations are often surrounded by growth investors who expect the company's future prospect (e.g., revenue and earnings) to grow drastically and use current results and research to justify the investment decision by ignoring past key data by which track records can hardly be traced. During the tech bubble, from 1995 to 2000, many investors thought that the technology industry was the so-called promised land, where fortunes could be made overnight. And so they were willing to pay very high prices for any company with a dot-com name. When the bubble burst, a huge amount of money was lost virtually overnight.

Conversely, value investors tend to focus on buying stocks of troubled companies at bargain prices by looking back at what has already happened (e.g., the company's past) for consistency. They use the latest results to calculate the company's intrinsic value and pay less attention to the qualitative side of the company. Once they

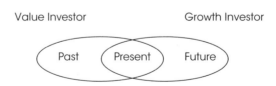

Figure 1.1   Difference in time horizon focus between a value investor and a growth investor

find a bargain, they will not hesitate to take action to buy into the company. Either way, both strategies can produce winners and losers in the long run.

At this point, do not mistakenly believe that all value investors operate this way. Benjamin Graham, for one, focused more on quantitative measurements compared to qualitative measurements when he analyzed a stock. However, over the past several decades, Warren Buffett, one of his students, has fine-tuned the investment process in such a way that it combines both the strategies of growth investing and value investing. This makes the whole investment process more effective and has proven to produce one of the best returns in town—one that enables Buffett to continuously outperform the overall market.

This investment process is what forms the basis of this book— value investing in growth companies where we look at quality growth companies that sell at bargain prices. In short, we call this strategy *value-growth investing*. In the remaining chapters, we will focus on these two methodologies to help you improve your returns in the long run. In doing so, we can combine these two strategies to create synergy, whereby the pros of each model are adopted and the cons are eliminated. This could give us a big advantage when it comes to investing in growth companies. With this combination, we have created a new type of investor, the value-growth investor, in which we deploy a strategy of using the value investing philosophy that has been improved upon over the past decades and applying them in growth companies.

Value-Growth Investors

Peter Lynch, who grew Fidelity's Magellan Fund from US$ 18 million in 1977 to more than US$14 billion in 1990, said in his book *One Up on Wall Street*, "Warren Buffett looks for the same sorts of opportunities I do, except that when he finds them, he buys the whole company." As you can tell, these two investors use a very similar technique for finding good growth companies and buying them at a bargain price—a

A stock can be undervalued and at the same time outperform to become a growth stock.

While many investors consider value and growth to be different approaches and think of themselves as either value or growth investors, we do not think of these two approaches as such. In our opinion, a stock can be undervalued and at the same time outperform to become a growth stock.

Figure 1.2   Examples of pure value investors, pure growth investors, and value-growth investors

combination of value and growth investing strategies works wonderfully well for them. It gives them a higher return on investment with lower risks.

> Value and growth are joined at the hip.
> —*Warren Buffett*

According to Buffett, "Value and growth are joined at the hip." In 1969, Buffett described himself as 85 percent Benjamin Graham (value investor) and 15 percent Fisher (growth investor). In the 1992 annual report of Berkshire Hathaway, he wrote, "The two approaches are joined at the hip: growth is always a component in the calculation of value, constituting a variable whose importance can range from negligible to enormous and whose impact can be negative as well as positive."

Today, as shown in the Figure 1.2, we believe Buffett gives equal attention to both qualitative and quantitative considerations, as he continues to fine-tune Graham's investment style when necessary, to produce consistent returns in the long run.

Now let us learn more about this legendary investor.

Warren Buffett's Journey

When he was in college, Buffett was taught value investing by Benjamin Graham. Thereafter, he moved to Omaha, where he started his own investment firm, Buffett Partnership, when Graham retired from the investment world. While running the investment partnership, Buffett realized that stocks that were undervalued continued to perform well in the long run. With this realization, Buffett started to fine-tune the purely quantitative value investing model developed by Graham.

He found that the underlying business continued to improve because the company's business model had some competitive advantages working in its favor long after Graham sold those shares. This made Buffett search for a better answer and allowed him to dig further, when he learned that qualitative factors attributed to growth stocks. He continued to search for books that placed an emphasis on the quality of a company. Eventually, his efforts paid off when he picked up Philip Fisher's *Common Stocks and Uncommon Profits* and learned about qualitative elements in growth investing.

Regarding his longtime partner, Charlie Munger, Buffett often credits Munger for having told him that "a great business at a fair price is superior to a fair business at a great price." Munger's and Fisher's insights into investment helped Buffett move from a pure Graham style of investing to one that focuses on great businesses with quality management. This is one reason why Buffett is able to beat Graham's record: He looks for good-quality businesses with consistent track records and trustworthy management and buys them at a fair, and sometimes at an undervalued, price.

Often people mistakenly believe Buffett to be a pure value investor. However, it is obvious that Buffett's style is actually a combination of value and growth investing. Some investors may call his style *growth at reasonable price* (GARP), but in this book, we call this approach *growth at undervalued price* (GAUP), because we found out many of the growth companies in Asia are trading below their intrinsic value.

Buffett shifted to GARP from pure value investing when he started his investment career with Graham. Now he is more focused on paying a fair price for a good company. In other words, good growth companies are neither too cheap nor too expensive. In Asia or any other part of the world, there is an abundance of opportunities in which one can find growth companies selling below their intrinsic value, regardless of the economic conditions. It is then really about having the right knowledge and technique to unearth these hidden gems.

Let us return to the subject of the time horizon. This time around, we will be focusing on the value-growth investors' time frame. This is a time frame that we, as value-growth investors, would spend studying a company in detail. Be it its past, present, or future growth, we will study them all to make sure that we know the company inside out before arriving at a decision as to whether it is a real growth company.

Value-Growth Investors

As shown in Figure 1.3, value-growth investors focus on a company's past, present, and future. We check the company's core business from the past to the future, to see if its core business remains unchanged. When we buy a stock, we are buying ownership of a company's business. In other words, we are becoming an owner, and it is important for us to understand the business's past as much as how the business would stay relevant with consumers in the next 10 to 20 years.

By owning a piece of business, we do not possess the right to operate it; we leave this job to the experts. So, who are these experts? Here the term refers to the management team that runs the show. It is important for us to ensure that the company is managed by candid, honest, and competent management, both in the past and in the present. Before we purchase a stock, we will project its core business into the future to see whether it is able to sustain itself and grow bigger. At the same time, we look at its current management, because the future success of the company is highly dependent on them. We also take into consideration the company's financial track record. When valuing it, we use the latest results to estimate and project earnings per share in the future, so as to determine how much the company is worth and how much the market price is at that moment. Figure 1.4 is a summary of what we look out for in a company in relation to time.

The beauty of this strategy is that it is applicable to both bear and bull markets. Our main objective is to find growth companies

Value-Growth Investor

Past   Present   Future

Figure 1.3   Value-growth investors focus on a company's past, present, and future

Past	Present	Future
Business		
Management		
Numbers		
	Valuation	

Figure 1.4   Value-growth investors' investment strategy with respect to time

at bargain prices. During bear markets, there is likely to be more bargain stocks for value-growth investors to choose from. Even during bull markets, there are still some undervalued stocks that one might find in Singapore or overseas markets, although there will be fewer of them than in bull markets.

The key rationale behind this book is simple—to buy good growth companies at bargain prices, when the business can continue to earn greater profitability. As the intrinsic value continues to increase as a result of higher earnings, the investment would become more and more undervalued compared to the price that was initially paid.

Definition of Growth Companies

From the start of this book, we have been talking about growth companies. But what exactly are growth companies? In this book, the terms *growth companies* and *fast-growing companies* are used interchangeably. Before we begin to explain what they are, we will first introduce a company's life cycle.

Companies have different life cycles, just as trees do. Each family of trees has its own life cycle. Some trees are born, mature, and die rapidly. Others, like bristlecone pine trees, have life cycles lasting thousands of years. Trees continually face threats to their survival. Sometimes these threats are natural and uncontrollable, like sudden changes in climate. However, some are man-made and controllable.

Just like trees, companies have different life cycles. A company may be a fast grower and then die off immediately, or its legacy could last decades, like General Electric, which has been around for more than 100 years. Companies might face certain threats during their life cycles, such as changes in the industry, or they may encounter an unexpected event that could bring the company down. While some threats are uncontrollable, some result from controllable events (e.g., temporary or a one-time event).

In any case, growth companies are those that are expected to do well in the future; they have been able to grow at 15 percent or more in revenue, profits, and cash flow for the last five consecutive years, as they have been able to find winning business formulas amid tough times. These companies carry more risks than the larger companies. Owing to their rapid growth during their initial stage of expansion, these companies tend to be highly unstable as their expansion plans might fail.

It is true that, by investing in fast-growing companies when they are still young, investors can make tons of money as the share prices are likely to appreciate when demand and investors' interest grows. However, for investors who are not equipped with the right knowledge to invest in fast-growing companies, this can prove to be very risky. Picking the wrong company can be damaging to your financial portfolio and cause you to lose a lot of money. In view of this fact, we have decided to share our experience and knowledge so that you can better invest in these young companies. In our opinion, it is very important for investors who seek substantial portfolio appreciation to own growth companies because they offer the greatest potential in the long run, given their outstanding growth rates.

Young companies, with small to medium market capitalizations, are some of the best-performing stocks during bull markets.

Historically, researchers have also shown that young companies, with small to medium market capitalizations, are some of the best-performing stocks during bull markets. In Asia's context, we estimate that the total capitalization of these companies tends to be less than US$1 billion.

Common Misconceptions about Growth Companies

Good growth stocks are not the hot stocks that you learn about from your friends, newspapers, or experts. Instead, they are out-of-favor stocks, unpopular and unwanted. Accumulating shares of out-of-favor stocks when they are not covered by analysts is likely to reap you a handsome reward when they become the next hot stock. In fact, research has shown that out-of-favor stocks that have very strong business fundamentals, beat the market in the long run.

In the stock market, investors like to look for the next hot stock to buy, with hopes that the stock price will keep going up, even though the fundamentals of the business are not sound. Typically, hot stocks are heavily covered by analysts from various brokerage firms. When they give the signal to buy, stock prices tend to shoot up and become overvalued. Such is an example of a bad growth company, which leads investors to mistakenly think that the company has a potential to become a hot stock. A bad growth company is not one in which the stock price has been dropping or that has been in the headlines for the wrong reasons. The following are some of the common myths concerning growth companies.

Myth 1: The Higher the Growth Rate, the Better the Company

An ideal fast-growing company grows at a comfortable rate of between 15 and 50 percent. Even so, companies must fulfill other criteria to be considered safe investments. By and large, there are two categories of growing companies to avoid:

1. Those mainly financed by debt
2. Those that might be cyclical companies

The first category comprises companies that are able to grow within the comfort range but are mainly financed by debts during their initial growing stage. These are companies that turn to debt to finance the business's expansion. The reason we avoid them is that when a crisis strikes, such companies are unlikely to survive it. Chances of them issuing additional shares at a discount, in order to pay off debt, are high. As a shareholder, this will dilute your holding. On top of that, the expansion that was financed by debt might not turn out to be successful. So, why should we invest in companies that are financed by debt? The reason is capital preservation, as it is always the first and foremost principle that we abide by in investing.

In the second instance, though some companies might have low or zero debt, their operations might be affected during an economic downturn. For instance, companies that are in the construction, shipping, and property industries have a cyclical element to them. We view these companies as nongrowth companies, as they are unlikely to sustain continuous growth rate when another recession hits. As value-growth investors, we want companies that are more recession resilient than economically dependent. Not many stocks will pass this test, but it's possible to find them.

The growth does not need to be linear. Some minor fluctuation is expected year over year, but over a period of five to ten years, the company should grow conservatively at a range of 15 to 50 percent. However, at anything beyond this rate, investors must be careful because the company might be considered a hot stock in a glamour industry. This leads us to the next myth.

Myth 2: Fast Growers Are Companies in Fast Growing Industries

When people think of growth stocks, they usually think of companies in a growing industry, like technology companies, such as Facebook, Samsung, Microsoft, Apple, and Cisco. This, however, is not true. Some of the growth stocks in Singapore, like Boustead, BreadTalk, Super Group, ARA Asset Management, and Japan Food, are not stocks considered to be in fast-growing industries, with a business presence across Asia. However, they have achieved a historical growth rate of more than 15 percent per year. This goes to show that it is not necessary for growth companies to be in a fast-growing industry. Rather, it is preferable for them to be in a slow-growing industry, as long as they have room for expansion. Even if they belong to a seemingly boring industry, such companies could give us a potential multibagger return when we buy them cheap, especially when they are still in their initial stages of growth. In short, industry does not affect our decision to classify a company as a growth stock.

Myth 3: You Cannot Buy Growth Companies at Bargain Prices

We will show you that there are many undervalued growth companies, especially during an economic crisis. However, some of the fast-growing companies are cheap for a reason. It might be that something is wrong with the company (e.g., disappointing quarterly results, loss of recent projects, a lawsuit, or failed products), so its share price may be stagnant for a very long period of time. However, by using the Jigsaw Puzzle Model, you will know how to seize the opportunity and make money even when the company is faced with temporary problems. Additionally, we will explain how to avoid companies confronted with problems that have a permanent effect on profitability.

Myth 4: Fast Growers Are Companies That Have Small Market Capitalization

Yes, this may be true for some, but not for all, fast-growing companies that have small market capitalization. Some large companies, like Noble Group, whose business is commodity related, had a market capitalization estimated at $3.3 billion in 2005 yet could still grow at a very fast rate. These fast-growing companies started with a small market capitalization, then morphed to possess large capitalizations, as the underlying businesses continue to grow when they successfully duplicate the business model overseas. Since growth companies are often small and unpopular, they are often ignored by investors due to their size. However, when they start to excel, they may gain traction with the analyst community and move onto the radar of hedge funds and institutional investors. Before the company reaches a market capitalization size that might attract institutional investors, our aim is to discover its potential and purchase quality stock at a discounted rate from its intrinsic value.

Some common disadvantages of small-capitalization stocks are low liquidity, resulting in stocks that are very hard to buy or sell and trade at a very low price, with a wide spread (i.e., a big gap between bidding and asking price).

With high liquidity, investors can easily trade the stock for a quick profit. This creates the ability to convert the stock into cash quickly. As such, it creates a temptation to trade more frequently. As growth companies (especially those with small capitalizations) tend to have a very low liquidity, we are forced to trade less frequently, given the fact that we are presented with fewer opportunities to sell after purchasing a stock.

Although liquidity is very important in the stock market and, unless you have large funds to deploy, it should not be viewed as a threat. Having said that, it is a double-edged sword: An investor will have the challenge of selling the stock if he

The goal of value growth investors is to buy growth companies that are performing well and to sell them once institutional investors step in and start to acquire these stocks.

realizes that he made a mistake in investing in the stock. Therefore, it is important for you to do your homework thoroughly before purchasing a stock.

Myth 5: Small and Fast-Growing Companies Are Not Covered by Analysts and Institutions

This is true in a market like that of the United States, because of the huge number of listed companies. However, in, say, Singapore, there were only around 700 companies, both on the main board and the secondary Catalist board, listed on the Singapore Exchange (SGX), in 2010. This number is rather small compared to the number of companies on the New York stock exchange or the Japanese Stock Exchange. Here, the total market capitalization is also very small relative to that of the larger exchanges.

In Singapore, there are many analysts who constantly study companies that are young and new as they have a very limited pool of companies to study. Thus, smaller-growth companies might be covered by some analysts, but are definitely not as popular, compared to a hot stock or blue-chip company.

Ultimately, the goal of value-growth investors is to buy growth companies that are performing well and to sell them once institutional investors step in and start to acquire these stocks. Even if it takes several years for the stocks to attract widespread attention, it would be worthwhile to buy, hold, and, at the same time, receive passive income. As institutional investors come on board, the share price is likely to be pushed higher due to huge demand and the amount of money being traded.

Myth 6: Growth Companies Pay Very Little Dividend

Many growth companies pay very little dividends, as they need to use the capital generated to reinvest in the business. On average, most growth companies pay out about 20 to 50 percent of their net earnings to shareholders as dividends. The retained earnings are channeled back into the business to run the day-to-day operations and expansion plans. However, when it comes to the calculation of a dividend yield, it can be very misleading, as it takes the latest dividend and divides it by the current market price. Thus, the percentage seems to be lower. However, when one holds the stocks of a company that continuously generates strong cash flow, dividend yield tends to increase year by year. The payout ratio could remain at 30 percent, or be more or less, based on the company's policy. However, if no new shares have been issued and, say, profit goes from $100 million to $150 million, dividend per share would increase by 50 percent.

For instance, when Investor A invests in a company at an undervalued price, say $0.50 per share, where the dividend per share is $0.025 per share, the dividend yield is 5 percent. As the company continues to grow, it increases the dividend to $0.05 in the following year. If Investor A continues to hold onto the stock, the dividend yield (based on his purchase price) will be 10 percent, assuming no new shares have been issued via warrant conversion, options, placement, or rights issue. In summary, the dividend yield growth is subject to future earnings, dividend payout ratio, and increase in issued shares. When the company excels, it may continue to increase its payout, unless it has other better opportunities to grow its earnings per share.

Why Value-Growth Investing?

As proven by Warren Buffett in his 1984 article "The Superinvestors of Graham-and-Doddsville," value-investing strategy applied to growing companies can outperform the market. In the article, Buffett mentioned some fund managers who used to work for Benjamin Graham or practiced value investing and achieved returns that beat the market in the long haul. Table 1.2 provides a list of such fund managers who have had above-average market returns.

Although value-growth investing is a slow way of realizing profits, over time, you should see a substantial gain in profits, if you

Table 1.2   Examples of fund managers who earned above-average market returns through value-growth investing

Fund Period	Manager	Period	No. of Years	Returns
TBK Limited Partners	Tom Knapp	1968–1983	16	20%
WJS Limited Partners	Walter J. Schloss	1956–1984	28	21.3%
Sequoia Fund, Inc.	William J. Ruane	1970–1984	13	18.2%
Pacific Partners, Ltd.	Rick Guerin	1965–1983	19	32.9%
Perlmeter Investments, Ltd.	Stan Perlmeter	1965–1983	19	23%
Charles Munger, Ltd.	Charles Munger	1962–1975	14	19.8%

learn to pick the right stocks. Value-growth investors' priorities are to limit capital losses, ensure capital preservation before any gain, and capital appreciation. It does not matter how long it takes us to realize our profit. For us, the chances of realizing a profit are high, as long as we have our facts right and do our homework.

In summary, there are two ways a value-growth investor can generate returns.

Capital Appreciation or Intrinsic Value Appreciation

This can be thought of as capital gains. A stock with a $1 trading price is said to have a gain of $0.20 when its stock price moves to $1.20. This is a 20 percent gain. When an undervalued stock is held in the long run, the stock price can reflect the fundamentals of the company. Besides, when a company continues to compound and increase its business at 15 percent per year, the value of the company should increase earnings over time, followed by increases in its intrinsic value. When we know how to determine its valuation, we are more likely to purchase a bargain stock and have greater returns through capital appreciation.

For example, by investing in Boustead Singapore, an engineering services and geospatial provider, in 2002 at S$0.20 per share, you would have enjoyed a 25 percent compounded return (excluding the dividend payout during eight years of holding) by 2010, with a trading price of S$1.20. That is a six-bagger with a return on investment (ROI) of 500 percent on your initial invested capital. In other words, S$10,000 (50,000 shares) invested with Boustead in 2002 will give you S$60,000 in capital gains alone!

Although there is an increase in the share price, it does not mean that the market has realized its intrinsic value. It does not worry us, even if it takes some time for the market to realize its true worth because, while holding onto growth companies, the intrinsic value could continue to appreciate over time with improved earnings. In this case, our money continues to compound at a rate that is growing. That being said, many investors do not realize this hidden growth in intrinsic value. For example, in 2003, the intrinsic value of Company A was $1 in the first year. Its business and management plans continued to work out well, and the company grew at rates of 10 to 20 percent per annum (p.a.). Ideally, the share price of the company should be as shown in Table 1.3.

Table 1.3   Share price of Company A over 5 years

Year	Company A @ 10% p.a. growth rate	Company A @ 20% p.a. growth rate
1	$1.00	$1.00
2	$1.10	$1.20
3	$1.21	$1.44
4	$1.33	$1.73
5	$1.46	$1.90

Five years later, the intrinsic value will have increased. Different growth rates will yield a different set of results. In reality, intrinsic value will have changed when a new set of results are announced and factored into the calculation. Thus, it is necessary to know whether the company would be able to sustain this growth rate.

As value-growth investors, we intend to invest long term. We search for undervalued growth companies. We find them when others (the offerer) have not. Usually, big firms like to acquire small- and medium-capitalization companies that have strong balance sheets and are growing rapidly. These are big firms that tend to have a larger market capitalization than the target firm to be merged or acquired by the company (merger and acquisition).

In theory, hearing that Company A is trying to take over Company B (which we own) is often both good and bad news. The good news is that Company A will offer a material premium price (to the current traded price) to entice all shareholders of Company B to accept the takeover bid. The bad news is that we will not be able to compound our money in the long run if the company is successfully acquired or privatized. In fact, we might be forced to sell our shares to them, which is a scenario that we do not want. In such a situation, it is not uncommon for us to receive a constant stream of letters urging us to accept the offer, simply because they are paying a premium price.

When we invested in Design Studio in June 2010, we were soon rewarded for unearthing this gem with an offer at a premium price that was higher than the original purchase price. We realized a 40 percent gain in two months (see Table 1.4). In this case, this company had been growing at more than 20 percent in revenue, net profits, and cash flow from 2006 to 2009.

Design Studio aside, another growth company was Thomson Medical Centre (TMC), acquired by Peter Lim. In this case, TMC was one of the growth companies that managed to increase its sales,

Table 1.4   Stock performance of Design Studio (ROI: 40% in two months)

Date	Status	Price	Remarks
10 June 2010	BUY	S$0.45	
28 June 2010	HOLD	S$0.55	Depa made cash offer
2 August 2010	HOLD	S$0.65	Depa revised offer price

Table 1.5   Stock performance of Thomson Medical Centre (ROI: 337.5% in two years)

Date	Status	Price	Remarks
March 2009	BUY	S$0.40	
Oct 2009	HOLD	S$1.00	Economy recovering
Nov 2010	SELL	S$1.75	Peter Lim made cash offer

net profits, and cash flow at more than 16 percent from 2004 to 2009. If you had discovered this company during the downturn, it would have been highly lucrative. In general, this type of company tends to be recession resilient (like supermarkets and utilities), as it is in the healthcare industry and able to maintain steady growth rates. In 2009, you could have easily bought its share at a price of S$0.40. In October 2010, the offerer announced his intent to buy this company at a premium price of S$1.75. Investors were well rewarded with an ROI of 337.5 percent within two years (see Table 1.5).

Another growth company was Eng Kong, a container service company that grew at more than 17 percent annually and was acquired by Navis Capitalisation Partner at a premium price of 37 percent, based on the last transacted price. If you had invested in this company in 2009, your gain would have been even more, when the price was hovering at around S$0.10. They finally acquired this company at S$0.295, representing an ROI of 195 percent within two years (see Table 1.6).

Shareholders of Singapore Petroleum Company (SPC) were also well rewarded when PetroChina announced its wish to acquire SPC at S$6.25 per share in cash in June 2009. In January 2009, its shares were trading at S$2.84. This is an ROI of 120 percent within six months (see Table 1.7). From 2002 to 2006, SPC was able to increase its business at a compounded rate of more than

Table 1.6   Stock performance of Eng Kong (ROI: 195% in two years)

Date	Status	Price	Remarks
February 2009	BUY	S$0.100	
January 2010	HOLD	S$0.200	Economy recovering
June 2010	SELL	S$0.295	Navis made cash offer

Table 1.7   Stock performance of Singapore Petroleum Company (ROI: 120% in six months)

Date	Status	Price	Remarks
January 2009	BUY	S$2.84	
March 2009	HOLD	S$4.00	Economy recovering
June 2009	SELL	S$6.25	PetroChina made cash offer

30 percent before it was fully acquired by PetroChina! As shown, all of these companies have the same characteristics—they grew at more than 15 percent per year, with strong balance sheets and negligible debts.

Sometimes, companies compete with one another to take over a target company. This was what happened to Parkway Holding. As we have seen, if you own shares in a company that is subject to a bidding war, you are likely to gain more substantial profits from your investment. In this case, both Fortis and Khazanah wanted to use Parkway, which runs hospitals in Singapore, Malaysia, India, and China, to spearhead their regional expansion in healthcare. The bidding price was at its high of S$3.80 per share before it was being delisted. In late 2009, the price was trading at less than S$2. So, if you had invested in Parkway earlier, you could have doubled your capital within a year! That said, our intention is not to find a growth stock and hope that some potential buyer acquires it. Instead, we are more interested in finding companies that are able to compound our money.

Dividend Growth and Passive Incomes

When it comes to ROIs most investors focus on capital gains alone and overlook dividend growth and passive incomes. That is owing to some returns that short-term traders are unlikely to benefit from—dividends. Yet this is the secret to earning passive income.

Table 1.8   Dividend yield to grow from 5% to 12% from 2005 to 2010

Year	2005	2006	2007	2008	2009	2010
Dividend per Share (cents)	5.00	6.00	7.00	10.00	11.00	12.00
Market Price ($)	1.00	1.20	1.40	2.00	2.10	2.50
Dividend Yield at Market Price (%)	5.00	5.00	5.00	5.00	5.00	5.00
Dividend Yield at $1 (%)	5.00	6.00	7.00	10.00	11.00	12.00

When investors buy a share below its intrinsic value, the dividend yield tends to be very high when the market has mispriced it during a crisis or when the company is faced with bad news. As earnings and cash flow continue to improve, the company should pay out generous dividends (say, at 5 percent) based on its current depressed price. However, as a value-growth investor, we buy into the company at a low price and continue to hold it in the long run, for a period of, say, five years. By doing so, this could allow the dividend yield to grow from 5 to 12 percent between a period, for example, from 2005 to 2010 (see Table 1.8), which is then measured against the initial purchase price of $1. (Caveat: no increase in shares in issue, payout stays constant or increases, as mentioned earlier.)

As you can see, the dividend, when compounded over time, would yield the best return for long-term investors. The math tells you that, in the long run, dividend growth is worth a lot (provided the company consistently delivers earnings growth of more than 15 percent). Thus, buying and holding winners proves to be truly rewarding to value-growth investors. Most investors are short term, or do not have the patience to hold on for the long run to benefit from it. The best part is that, as long as the company continues to pay out dividends, prices of its stocks would continue to appreciate over time. However, to invest in such companies, they should be fundamentally strong and cash rich to withstand tough times.

When investors buy a company that is undervalued, the dividend that is calculated tends to be more than 5 percent. This, however, might not be the same when the company starts to pay out more dividends as it grows bigger in size.

Growth stocks do pay out very good dividends when held in the long run.

Imagine for a moment that you bought a company with an intrinsic value of $2 and a dividend of $0.05. The price you paid to get this company had a margin of safety of 50 percent, meaning that you paid $1 to acquire a stake in this company. Now, that is a 5 percent dividend yield. As the company's intrinsic value continues to improve due to growth in sales and net profit, the company decides to double its dividend payout because it has achieved a strong set of results the following year. That could have given you a dividend yield of 10 percent (provided shares in issue remain constant). This actually happened, in the case of Boustead. For instance, from the previous example, an investment of S$10,000 in 2002 could give you around 50,000 shares with the share price of S$0.20 per share. The calculated dividend yield based on S$0.20 bought in 2002 is shown in Table 1.9. Its growth in dividend yield increased from 3.7 to 27.5 percent in 2010.

In other words, you would have received dividends *consistently* from Boustead every year if you had continued to hold the shares until 2010. This comes to a total dividend of about S$11,845! And this is purely passive income! Obviously, if you are to buy a growth company when it is somewhat cheap, you could wind up doing better than growth investors who have paid a premium price. However, it must be said that we are not recommending Boustead to you. Instead, the key lesson here is that growth stocks do pay out very good dividends when held in the long run; this happened to Boustead when it hit its growth stage. Having said that, we strongly believe value-growth investing is a low-risk approach to investing.

Table 1.9   Dividend yield based on $0.20 bought in 2002 (Boustead Singapore)

Year	2003	2004	2005	2006	2007	2008	2009	2010
Dividend per Share (cents)	0.75	0.75	1.50	2.94	3.25	5.00	4.00	5.50
Dividend at 50,000 shares (S$)	375.00	375.00	750.00	1,470.00	1,625.00	2,500.00	2,000.00	2,750.00
Dividend Yield (%)	3.70	3.70	7.50	14.70	16.20	25.00	20.00	27.50

In general, there are a few ways in which you can lose money in the stock market when the companies you invest in are:

1. Bankrupt from being highly leveraged from banks (margin call)
2. Reporting consecutive net losses (prices would drop)
3. Bought at a high price/overvalued

With these factors in mind, it is easy to see why growth companies are commonly thought to be one of the riskiest investments. As a value-growth investor, you know how to avoid these costly mistakes, which could potentially burn your wealth away, simply because you know how to read annual reports and, in doing so, eliminate companies that are highly leveraged (except those in the property industry) or have incurred a loss for the past few years. You would also not pay for a company if it is overvalued. In relation to this, it must be said that it is not difficult to find promising growth stocks and pay below their intrinsic value. You need to find potential growth companies with simple and easy-to-understand business models, a management team that you can trust, and a strong balance sheet. Companies that fulfill these basic criteria are likely to survive a crisis, because they have no debt and have sufficient cash to tide them through tough times.

We shall be teaching you more about this in the chapters to come. Let us move on!

Summary

- Do not go into short-term trading if you have a full-time business or job. This is a common pitfall for young or start-up investors.
- Be a long-term investor, as you will have more time for other activities.
- Characteristics of good-growth companies:
  - Growth rate: 15 to 50 percent over five years
  - Not necessary to be in a growing industry
  - Not too highly geared to finance its expansion and produce modest profit returns to shareholders
  - Have market capitalization below US$1 billion, although not all fall under this guideline

- ◆ Possible to purchase at undervalued prices
- ◆ Less covered or studied by institutional investors and analysts
- ◆ Have higher risks than blue-chip companies. The risks could be reduced when you understand the company thoroughly
- ◆ Are more prone to be taken over by bigger companies
- Value-growth investors would benefit from capital gains and receive good dividends by holding good-growth companies in the long run.

The Secrets of Successful Value-Growth Investors

Healthy Thoughts Lead to Sustainable Results

There are no secrets to being a successful value-growth investor. Moreover, secrets are no longer secrets once they are revealed. However, we can tell you one thing that is very important in order to become a successful value-growth investor, which is to develop the correct mindset before investing. We refer to the habits that we have practiced since day one of our investing journey. Before investing, you must understand how successful value-growth investors are wired and programmed. Successful investing is more than simply knowing all about stocks. Understanding yourself is equally important. Investors who make mistakes are those who allow their emotions to control their decisions, which is one of our biggest enemies when it comes to investing. Aside from our emotions, we must have a proper financial plan to allocate our money for investment. By developing such a mindset, as well as other mindsets that we are about to share, you should be able to enjoy consistent compounded annual returns.

Mindset 1: Understand the Power of Compound Interest

You need to comprehend the simple principle of compound interest, as it is the essence of wealth creation. By understanding compound interest, you will appreciate how long-term investors like Warren Buffett make billions by holding winning investments in the long run and generating many times their initial capital. You will be astonished by the way in which a single penny that you save, instead of spend, can grow into hundreds of dollars if invested to provide consistent and high compounded rates of return in the long run. You will also learn that this is one of greatest investment gains you can make.

By and large, the road to successful investing is based on the compounding effect—the longer one holds, the more significant the effect of compounding becomes. With this understanding, you are likely to be more patient, because you know that your money is working hard for you.

In fact, we have learned the basics of this during mathematics lessons in secondary school. Looking back, secondary mathematics provided us with good foundation to allow us to better comprehend our finances later in life. However, many of us have forgotten these basics. So let us recap the formula for compound interest:

$$A = P \times (1 + r)^n$$

Where:

   A = Amount of Money Accumulated after n Years
   P = Principal Capital ($)
   r = Annual Rate of Return n = Number of Years

This formula is not meant to intimidate you. Instead, it is for you to understand how compound interest works. As you can see from the formula, you need to have P—principal capital—in order for compound interest to work. Here, the term principal capital refers to the amount of starting cash that you set aside to invest. The next variable to note is the letter in the parentheses, r—the annual rate of return. This is the rate you wish to have the money compounded at a certain percentage.

The next variable to note is the power n—it is number of years you intend to hold the initial capital at a compounding interest rate.

For example: $P = \$1$, $R = 0.20$ (which is 20%), $n = 20$ years

From the formula,

$$A = P \times (1 + r)^n$$
$$A = \$1 \times (1 + 0.20)^{20}$$
$$= \$38.33$$

From the answers, we can see that every $1 compounded at a rate of 20% will grow to $38.33 in 20 years. Now let us provide you with another example to help you better understand the principle of compound interests.

Assume Investor A invests $500 a year, for 10 years, from the age of 21 to 30. He stops investing when he gets married and wants to buy a house. Investor B has more streams of income and has invested about $1,000 a year for 10 years, since the age of 31. In this case, Investor B starts to invest at a later age. Meanwhile, Investor C allocates money to invest at the age of 41 and contributes about $1,000 a year consistently, believing that it is never too late to invest.

When we were writing this book, Warren Buffett has personally generated a compounded rate of return of more than 20%. Peter Lynch has had a similar track record, compounding at more than 30% per annum. For our hypothetical investors, who may not be the next Warren Buffett or Peter Lynch, we shall assume that their compounded returns are much lower than those of these successful gurus and place it at 15%. The result of their investments is shown in Table 2.1.

From Table 2.1, it is obvious that the small contribution of $5,000 from Investor A helped him to accumulate a higher net return than Investors B and C, whose total contributions are $10,000 and $20,000 respectively. Surprisingly, Investor A realized a return of $767,933, excluding initial investment, even though he contributed less, compared to Investor B. In this case, Investor B contributed twice the initial capital but only realized a return of $372,132, representing about half of Investor A's return. Meanwhile, Investor C only had a net return of about $97,809.

With this information, we can conclude that there are two requirements for compound interest to work beautifully:

1. Time—The more time you have, the greater the compounding effect.
2. Money—The more money you invest at an early stage, the more money you get.

It is important for value-growth investors to understand this first mindset, as it serves as a foundation for the second mindset, which we will cover next.

Table 2.1   Investors' net return based on the principle of compound interest

	Investor A		Investor B		Investor C	
Age	Annual Contribution ($)	Amount	Annual Contribution ($)	Amount	Annual Contribution ($)	Amount
21	500	575	–	–	–	–
22	500	1236	–	–	–	–
23	500	1996	–	–	–	–
24	500	2871	–	–	–	–
25	500	3876	–	–	–	–
26	500	5033	–	–	–	–
27	500	6363	–	–	–	–
28	500	7893	–	–	–	–
29	500	10,151	–	–	–	–
30	–	11,674	–	–	–	–
31	–	13,425	1,000	1,150	–	–
32	–	15,438	1,000	2,472	–	–
33	–	17,754	1,000	3,993	–	–
34	–	20,417	1,000	5,742	–	–
35	–	23,480	1,000	7,753	–	–
36	–	27,002	1,000	10,066	–	
37	–	31,052	1,000	12,725	–	–
38	–	35,710	1,000	15,784	–	–
39	–	41,066	1,000	19,303	–	–
40	–	47,226	–	23,348	–	–
41	–	54,310	–	26,850	1,000	1,150
42	–	62,457	–	30,878	1,000	2,472
43	–	71,825	–	35,510	1,000	3,993
44	–	82,599	–	40,836	1,000	5,742
45	–	94,989	–	46,962	1,000	7,753
46	–	109,238	–	54,006	1,000	10,066
47	–	125,623	–	62,107	1,000	12,726
48	–	144,467	–	71,423	1,000	15,784
49	–	166,137	–	82,136	1,000	19,303
50	–	191,057	–	94,457	1,000	23,349
51	–	219,716	–	108,626	1,000	28,001
52	–	252,673	–	124,920	1,000	33,351
53	–	290,574	–	143,658	1,000	39,504
54	–	334,160	–	165,206	1,000	46,580
55	–	384,284	–	189,987	1,000	54,717
56	–	441,927	–	218,485	1,000	64,075

| | Investor A | | Investor B | | Investor C | |
Age	Annual Contribution ($)	Amount	Annual Contribution ($)	Amount	Annual Contribution ($)	Amount
57	–	508,216	–	251,258	1,000	74,836
58	–	584,448	–	288,946	1,000	87,211
59	–	672,116	–	332,289	1,000	101,443
60	–	772,933	–	382,132	1,000	117,809
Total	5,000	–	10,000	–	20,000	–
Net Return		767,933		372,132		97,809

Mindset 2: Start Young!

According to Benjamin Franklin, "Time is money." This statement certainly holds true when it comes to investing. The main reason that Investor A received more than Investor B and C is time. For Investor A, time is on his side. The earlier you start to invest, the better it is. You can take higher risks by investing in growth companies and afford to make more mistakes. You will still have sufficient time to turn things around if you learn from mistakes made along the way.

The net returns in Table 2.1 were calculated only up to 60 years old. However, according to figures published by the Singapore Department of Statistics, the life expectancy of the average Singaporean is 81.5 years. Life expectancy has been increasing since 1970, due to improvements in health and welfare. Women, on average, can expect to live longer than men by 4.7 years.

Using the example, Investor A started investing at a younger age than Investors B and C and, by doing so, earned higher net returns. This goes to show that younger investors have a bigger advantage over the older investors—the earlier one starts to invest, the better the principle of compound interest works for you in the long run. However, it is not too late for you to invest if you are like Investor B. At the very least, you have a big advantage over Investor A, as you are likely to be more established in your career and thus have more money to invest than those who are younger. If you are like Investor C, we are impressed by your persistence in pursuing wealth and security. This is indeed admirable. Although we are unable to control time, this book will also do you good, as it will help you make investment decisions based on simple and easy concepts. We also recommend you pass this book, the greatest gift of investment knowledge, to your kids or grandchildren. We believe they could benefit a lot from this book as they have the greatest, yet most scarce, resource on planet earth—time.

However, time without financial management knowledge is equally useless. At this stage, you might be under the impression that successful investors started with huge amounts of capital in order to get rich. However, not all of them had family fortunes; some of them started with very little capital to invest. It is never too late for you to start investing, even if you do not have a lot of savings. In that case, you need to manage your personal finances better.

Money surplus generated from your salary or business will go into a bank savings account after deducting basic expenses. According to the Singapore Statistics Department, the average inflation rate in Singapore was 2.1% from 1980 to 2009. The sad truth is that the money you saved in 1980 will not be worth as much today. Its value gets eroded at a rate of 2.10% annually. This has been worse in the recent years, when inflation reached 5% in the first quarter of 2011. In view of rising inflation, value-growth investors must do more to be able to keep, preserve, and watch their money grow. The best way to compound your money is to invest it in the right investment vehicles and, we hope, watch it grow year after year. By doing so, you need not start your own business but tap into someone else's talent for running a business by buying some shares in that company. And that is really why we invest.

Needless to say, there are people who have trouble saving money; they will understandably have lots of excuses for it. Whatever it is, it is always better to delay instant gratification and start saving. A dollar spent on something that you do not need but want could be equivalent to $38 in 20 years, compounded at a rate of 20%, if you invest it. For instance, the average price of a cup of bubble tea in Singapore is S$3.50. If you invested that amount it instead, the future value could have grown to S$133 (3.5 × S$38).

Smart value-growth investors reinvest all the dividends they receive to allow them to compound further.

Simply stated, you are spending S$133 on a cup of bubble tea. That is insane!

So, if you are ready to invest, our advice to you is to set aside the amount of money that you would not need until at least 10 to 20 years later. This would not affect the rate of return, as you might need some cash for your kids' education or as an emergency fund. A good rule of thumb is to set aside a minimum of 10% of your monthly salary or business cash flow to invest in stocks if you want to retire comfortably. Spending whatever you have will not make you rich. In fact, it could make you poorer, when you buy things on credit (e.g., cars). Successful value-growth investors choose to work hard now and enjoy later by delaying instant gratification. Better still, smart value-growth investors reinvest all the dividends they receive to allow the money to compound further. It is truly a plus if you have existing investments that generate some passive income every year.

Mindset 3: Be a Long-Term Investor!

As explained in Mindset 1, it is much easier to invest in the long run, because you have more time to let the effect of compound interest take shape. We shall now explore this point further, to further convince you of the need to hold the right investments in the long run.

The strategy of long-term investing has been proven for decades. For instance, let's say you bought the Singapore STI index in 1988 and held it until 2010. The index peaked at over 3,800 points in the last quarter of 2007, before the financial crisis hit. If you were to compound this for a period of 19 years, it would amount to a 7.8% compounded return. Even at its lowest point of around 1,500 points during the 2008–2009 financial crisis, your initial investment would still be generating more than 2.7% compounded return after 20 years. In fact, at the time of writing this book, the STI had rebounded back to 3,000 points. In Malaysia, KLCI has generated compounded return of around 7% over the last 14 years. After more than two and half decades, in China, the Hang Seng Index has generated overall compounded return of around 8%. We can go on and on, but what does this tell us? Without a doubt, long-term investing is arguably a sound strategy with merit.

You might be intrigued as to why value-growth investors do not operate in the short term. The definition of short-term investment is investment held for less than a year. As a short-term investor, one has to be able to take high risks in the stock market due to its high volatility. Short-term investors often look out for quick cash in the shortest time, ranging from a few hours, days, weeks, to a few months, by timing the market as to when to buy and sell. Most investors who try to time the market end up buying high and selling low. Remember, every $1 would be worth $38 in future value if compounded by 20% over a period of 20 years. So, if you are to trade 10 times a month, with an average cost per trade of $30, the total cost will amount to $11,400 (10 × $30 × $38) in commission fees that you pay to your broker every month. But if you are look-ing short, you obviously cannot see this compounding effect. In view of this, it is probably best to trade less to make more money with less activity.

In summary, while the stock market is unpredictable in the short term, it becomes predictable in the long term. Nothing is more valuable than being invested in a growth company and enjoy-ing compounded returns that are above the market's average. Buffett's holding period, as he famously said, is forever. He has confessed that he makes more money by snoring than by working. Long-term thinking is essential because short-term volatility can-not be consistently predicted. In the long run, the stock market is a wealth creator! This explains Buffett's tremendous success; he is a long-term investor.

Mindset 4: Never Leverage to Invest in the Long Run!

Applying Mindset 3—being a long-term investor—would not guar-antee success if you invest with borrowed money. As value-growth investors, we will devote some time to analyzing and studying the company's business, assessing the quality of its management, and looking at numbers before we are willing to pay a specific price for that company. In doing so, we want to know how the company would grow in future.

This requires effort and time to ensure success.

If you trade 10 times a month, with an average cost per trade of $30, the total cost will amount to $11,400 in commission fees.

Since time is a big consid-eration for us to hold an invest-ment in the long run, it is recommended that you do not borrow money to invest.

Say no to borrowing money when it comes to investing (unless it is a mortgage or investment property, but that is beyond the scope of this book). We do not want to invest in companies that are highly financed by debt to run their daily operations because, when a crisis hits the company, it is unlikely that the company will pay off its debt. Likewise, we do not want to invest in companies by borrowing money from the bank because a bank can recall the loan before our stock has realized its full potential. When that happens, we stand to lose a significant amount when we are forced to sell our stocks at the wrong time, in order to raise the necessary cash.

Instead of buying a business at a cheaper price, borrowing money to invest in the stock could force your good-growth company to become a great bargain for others who use their own cash to invest. Why? When you buy undervalued stocks, they might drop further before the market realizes their real value (say in the next five years). In the meantime, you are forced to sell it at a lower price in order to cover the debt owed to the bank.

Buffett's holding period, as he famously said, is forever. He has confessed that he makes more money by snoring than by working.

This is not even factoring in the interest rate charged on the amount of the loan. Say, for example, you borrow money to invest in a particular stock that you intend to hold in the long run. The bank charges you an annual interest rate of 5%. You decide to borrow $50,000 on top of your initial capital of $50,000, making your total invested capital $100,000.

- Scenario 1: When the economy is good, let us assume you make money at a 50% return on investment.
- Scenario 2: When the economy is flat, let us assume the price stays the same.
- Scenario 3: When the economy is in recession, let us assume you lose 50% of your invested capital.

As you can see from Table 2.2, within the first year, your investment makes a total gain of $45,000, after deducting your initial invested capital of $50,000, when the economy is good. This is a 90% return, and your return is amplified many more times. Having said that, investors often forget to think about what would happen if things do not go as planned. Under Scenarios 2 and 3, when the

Table 2.2 Total gain on investment when the economy is good, flat, or in recession

Scenario Currency	1 US$	2 US$	3 US$
Starting Capital	100,000	100,000	100,000
Ending Capital	150,000	100,000	50,000
Less Interest Rate (5%)	5,000	5,000	5,000
Less Return of Borrowing	50,000	50,000	50,000
Less Original Capital	50,000	50,000	50,000
Net Gain/Loss	45,000	−5,000	−55,000
Total Gain (%)	90	−10	−110

price breaks even or declines, you would suffer a negative return of $5,000 and $55,000 respectively.

In relation to this point, leverage is also commonly perceived to be a double-edged sword. So, when the economy rebounds, you are unlikely to enjoy its upside, since the bank has recalled all your personal assets due to your inability to pay off the debt with cash. Successful value-growth investors must be able to stay in the game for many years in order for their money to compound. When you invest without borrowing, free from financial burdens, you will live happily thereafter.

Mindset 5: Exercise Independent Thinking

Although you have successfully made the decision to invest in the long run, after learning about all its benefits as highlighted in the book, successful investing is really easier said than done, owing to all the market noise. By market noise, we are referring to so-called hot tips. Whether it comes from your friends, brother-in-law, or broker, you must learn to ignore them. In today's day and age, when investors are bombarded with tons of information from the radio, newspaper, and television, it often does more harm than good if investors simply follow unsolicited advice. Relying solely on these tidbits of information would not help you become a long-term investor. With more information than we need these days, it is easy for investors to fall into the hot tips trap, especially when they hear that a hot stock will jump overnight from, say, $0.50 to $2. They quickly invest all their hard-earned cash in order to get rich quick. And when you ask them why they purchased that stock, they will not have any substantial reason, except that somebody said they should. In such cases, their investments are purely speculative or mere gambles. In our opinion, your odds would probably be better at the casino.

Speaking of casinos, when the government announced the introduction of Integrated Resorts in Singapore, Genting stocks, which traded at S$1 in the first quarter of 2010, soon became hot stocks. Many people made money when its share price moved up to S$2, thereby doubling their investments. However, would this growth be sustainable in the future? This concern is actually not unfounded, given that it has a debt of about S$4 billion that has to be paid off in the future. Owing to the high risks involved as well as legalized gambling, which is something that goes against our value system, Genting is definitely not on our watch list.

When Warren Buffett was advised by Bill Gates to invest in one of the most profitable technology firms—Microsoft—Buffett exercised independent thinking and refused to invest in the technology sector, as he did not understand it. Instead, he preferred brick-and-mortar businesses. Because of this decision, he avoided potential losses when the dot-com crash took place in 2000. From this example, it goes to show that in order to become a successful investor, you must also have faith in your own research—the facts. In relation to this, we will teach you how to uncover facts to help in your decision making as to whether to buy or sell a particular stock. In doing so, you will learn that successful companies are the ones with hard facts that can prove themselves in the long run. In the short term, we may look foolish, as you are unlikely to see any positive returns in the first few weeks or months. However, in the long run, you would be well rewarded.

Put simply, think independently when it comes to making investment decisions. For every decision you make, you hold full ownership and responsibility.

Mindset 6: Be Emotionally Stable

Ideally, share price movement of a company should move in the direction of the true value arrow, as long as the business continues to receive an influx of earnings and cash flow. However, when human emotions are factored into the stock market, share price movement of a company is as reflected in Figure 2.1.

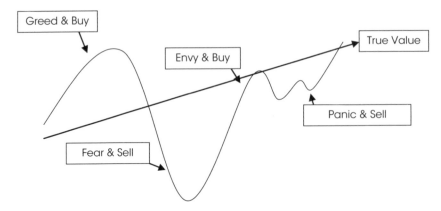

Exhibit 2.1 Share price movement and human emotions

We cannot help but have emotional responses. Seeing stock prices rise as the economy recovers, we are often tempted to enter the market, owing to our desire to make some quick money. Conversely, when we are confronted with danger, we will feel fear and interpret this as a signal to flee for safety's sake. Such fear is real when we start to see stock prices plunge. In such instances, investors will quickly sell for fear that the prices will fall further, in order to cut their losses. Letting your emotions dictate your investment strategies is not recommended. Succumbing to fear will cause great harm if you let it dictate buying and selling activities on the stock market, as it is often misleading. Instead, it is important for you to practice emotional stability in the stock market. Put simply, be rational instead of emotional.

Besides fear and greed, you have to control other emotions, such as anger and envy. Having said that, it is natural to be envious of others' success when they make money in the stock market, but when envy starts influencing our judgment, we tend to make investment mistakes. We also should not react with frustration to short-term changes in the market or our portfolio should things go against us.

In relation to this, we simply disagree with those who say, "Do not be greedy and expect the stock price to increase further. Your investment has already made money, it is time to sell and take the profits." If you buy a stock and it quickly jumps in price, it is natural for you to be tempted to sell it, lock in the profit, and go out and brag to others about your quick profit. But if you know that the company is still priced below its true value, why would you want to sell it? Surely, to do so, you must have a better logical, rather than emotional, reason to sell.

Using price as an indicator as to whether to sell is not a good idea. Just because you buy it cheaper does not mean that you have to sell it when its price goes up. Conversely, if the stock price falls, do not panic! You must look at the bigger picture.

Instead of being caught in the inevitable volatility of the market, be confident in the quality of your findings. Instead of focusing on day-to-day or even minute-to-minute market fluctuations (this is what short-term traders do), you should think of the long-term value of the company, even when its price fluctuates from year to year. For such reasons, it is important that you think long term rather than short term.

Understanding that short-term market fluctuations are part and parcel of every investment, we do not let our emotions or the market decides when we should buy. Instead, we make decisions based on facts. When we buy shares for $0.50 that we have determined should have an intrinsic value of $1, we do not panic when their price drops to $0.20. In fact, we would buy even more if all the facts and reasoning are still valid. In relation to this theory, Buffett's approach to the market is "As far as I am concerned, the stock market doesn't exist. It is there only as a reference to see if anybody is offering to do anything foolish."

The best way to get rid of our emotions in the stock market, as Buffett suggests, is to think that the market is not around. By this, he means that we should only buy a stock when we are perfectly happy to hold it, even if the stock market shuts down for the next decade. Put simply, a successful value-growth investor does not bring emotions into the stock market.

Mindset 7: Think Contrarian When Investing

Often, friends tell us to buy stocks simply because everyone is buying them. This is called the *herd mentality*, which is extremely dangerous when investing. Needless to say, following what others are buying without doing your due diligence is definitely an expensive lesson to learn. In this case, it can be easy for you to be blinded by your emotions when you see others purchasing a particular

Exhibit 2.2   Three levels of danger when investment decisions are influenced by the herd mentality

stock and telling you how much they have earned. In such a situation, you have to curtail your emotions when assessing whether to purchase the stock. When herd mentality starts to influence your investment decisions, you will start to experience three levels of danger (see Figure 2.2).

> *Understanding that short-term market fluctuations are part and parcel of every investment, we do not let our emotions or the market decide when we should buy. Instead, we make decisions based on facts.*

First, self-doubt. When everyone is buying a stock, you will start doubting whether you are right in *not* buying the stock. This is especially true when everyone starts to earn while you are not. Second, fear. Fear is one of the common causes of herding. Naturally, you will start to feel the fear of losing out when you start doubting yourself. Once fear overtakes your decision making, you will start to follow the crowd and buy what they buy. Third, and finally, a bad decision is the end result. When faced with self-doubt and fear, your investment decision will not be logical. However, your decision should be made only because you have knowledge of the company and believe that it would do well; it should not be based on emotion or the herd mentality to buy.

Buying a stock based on herd mentality is an absolute *no*. You have to start doing things differently from others. Warren Buffett, Peter Lynch, and John Neff earned their fortunes because they did things differently. They like to make use of market fear and greed, turning it to their advantage by being contrarian. They exploit market psychology by buying when everyone is fearful and selling. Such is their investment philosophy. Warren Buffett said, "Be fearful when others are greedy. Be greedy when others are fearful."

In order to become a successful value-growth investor, you must adopt a contrarian way of thinking—also called contrarian *investing*. This is a strategy that runs opposite to the majority's view. In other words, the 2008–09 crash created opportunities but also created fear around the world. People fled the equity market and dumped shares. It is at times like these that we must know how to exploit such great buying opportunities.

Additionally, these opportunities are often found in companies that are operating in a seemingly boring line of business, one that people seldom talk about or even bother to look at. It is useful to find great growth companies before they are discovered and thought to be the next big stock. In layman's terms, we buy stocks during an economic crisis, and other people think we are crazy. In their eyes, we might as well be catching a falling knife. Conversely, we would sell when everyone is talking about which specific stocks to buy or are rushing in to buy. The bottom line is, in order to prevent yourself from being influenced by the herd, do your due diligence in researching a company. Thereafter, you need to invest and stand firm by your decision.

Mindset 8: Understand Mr. Market (Efficient Market Theory versus Mr. Market)

The efficient market hypothesis is a modern financial theory developed by Eugene Fama in 1970. This hypothesis says, "It is impossible to beat the market because the price already incorporates and reflects all relevant information as soon as it becomes freely available." This means when information about a stock is available to one investor, it will become freely available to all investors at the same time. Therefore, the price of a stock will immediately reflect the knowledge and expectations of all investors, As a result, there is no way for investors to beat the market, since there is no way for them to know something about the stock that is not already reflected in the stock price, apart from insider information and insider trading, which is illegal. In other words, investors who believe this theory are told they should not try to pick winners, because stock values are always traded at their fair value and it is impossible to buy stocks at a bargain price (that is, those that are undervalued). As such, investors are engaging in a game of chance, not skill.

> Be fearful when others are greedy. Be greedy when others are fearful.
>
> —*Warren Buffett*

In reality, this theory is flawed, because all investors access information at different times and from different sources. Moreover, buyers often overreact to good news and vice versa. To address this issue, we would like introduce a concept that was developed by Benjamin Graham called *Mr. Market*, which could change the way you look at price. If employed correctly, it is likely to make you a successful value-growth investor.

So, who is Mr. Market? Mr. Market is a character that Graham used to explain his concept of the market in simpler terms. Imagine that you and Mr. Market are in a 50–50 partnership in a company. Every day, without fail, he offers to either buy your share of the company or sell you an additional share of the business at a specific price. Sometimes, the price might be reasonable and sometimes not, depending on his mood. The best part of Mr. Market is that he will not take offense if you choose to ignore him. Instead, he will come back to you another day with a new offer price. As you can see, although Mr. Market's mood is highly unstable, your 50% stake in the company is not affected. If you are investing from a business perspective, you will ignore Mr. Market until you are done with your homework and buy the share at a bargain price. Otherwise, you can sell your shares at a higher price. As Graham said, "Mr. Market is there to serve you, not to guide you." Mr. Market also hates bad news when the business is operating in a period of uncertainty or in a difficult operating environment.

Many quality growth companies were hit hard during the financial crisis from 2008 to 2009. When the STI dropped from approximately 3,800 points all the way to 1,500 points, the majority of companies' share prices were badly affected. And, understandably, Mr. Market was having his mood swing then. Share prices plummeted, even though business fundamentals and practices did not change. It caused the gap between market price and business value to widen. As such, there were more undervalued growth stocks than there were fairly valued ones (blue-chip companies). And value-growth investors were jumping in during that period to scoop up shares that were on sale. Worldwide sales!

For example, Hsu Fu Chi, a candy maker in China, continued to achieve strong sales growth despite the recession. In this case, the intrinsic value was S$1.10, while the market was quoting only S$0.60, with a margin of safety of more than 50 percent (including the net cash per share). Boustead was trading at S$0.46, when it had an intrinsic value of S$1.61, therein representing a margin of safety of more than 75 percent! Indeed, what a huge opportunity it was for value-growth investors to enter the market and scoop up quality stocks at bargain prices!

That said, the key lesson is not to be fooled by Mr. Market's irrational behavior; instead you can take advantage of him after you have done your homework (value). Remember, price is what you pay; value is what you get. In this case, Mr. Market is there for you to buy at good prices and sell at unreasonable prices. So, take advantage of it! Good growth companies will go up in value even during a bear market. The main point is to know that in the long run, the market is a weighing machine based on facts. In the short run, however, it is a voting machine based on market sentiments (e.g., fear or greed).

In conclusion, a successful value-growth investor must have patience when it comes to investing. In fact, patient is a virtue to us. However, there are many investors who are still out there searching for a book with a secret formula to acquire instant wealth. This secret formula, as revealed in this chapter, is patience.

There is a catch to being long-term investors; it may take as long as three to five years for us to be rewarded. We also have to delay instant gratification by not selling as soon as our stocks realize a profit. Instead, it is far more logical and profitable to sell based on the strategy that we are going to cover in the chapters to come. While waiting patiently for the money to compound, we also avoid unnecessary financial costs. We understand how not to jump off the ship too quickly by removing emotion from the decision-making equation.

Once you understand the concept of Mr. Market, as well as the market's ups and downs, you should know that there are opportunities awaiting us. In view of this, you must remember that the 2008–2009 crisis is not to be the last recession we will ever see; there will be more to come. We do not know when another financial crisis will happen and do not attempt to predict it. Just remember this simple saying: "After the rain, the sun will eventually shine again." After a recession, there will be a period of boom and vice versa.

Price is what you pay, value is what you get.

—*Warren Buffett*

If you still have a short-term trading mind-set, the next chapter is not for you. However, if you are able to master these habits of a successful value-growth investor, you are well on your way to becoming a true long-term investor; you think and invest long term by ignoring short-term price fluctuations.

There is more to learn in the following chapters, in which we discuss the intellectual framework needed for investment. It is going to be a bumpy ride sometimes, but it is definitely worthwhile. Once you understand the principles, it is really as easy as ABC.

Summary

- Successful investors choose to invest rather than let inflation erode their cash.
- Successful investors understand compound interest, and the importance of having more time and money, to create wealth.
- Successful investors start to allocate at least a minimum of 10 percent of their income to invest.
- Successful investors do not leverage to invest in equity, as the market is highly volatile.
- Successful investors know long-term investing works and will continue to work in the long run.
- Successful investors pay attention to value, not the day-to-day price fluctuations of stocks.
- Successful investors tend not to be emotional when it comes to stock prices, be it up or down by 50 percent; their emotions are relatively stable.
- Successful investors exercise independent thinking and make decisions based on facts.
- Successful investors think and act the opposite of the way the majority does—contrarian.
- Successful investors have patience!
- Successful investors are responsible for their own actions, and for any decision made, be it right or wrong.

CHAPTER 3

The Jigsaw Puzzle—Four Pieces to Value-Growth Investing

The Jigsaw Puzzle Model

In the previous chapter, you learned the importance of adopting the right mindset and temperament to become a successful value-growth investor. If you have yet to adopt them, we strongly advise you to internalize them before moving on to the next chapters. In any case, go over these proposed mindsets over and over again, so that they become the very essence of your long-term investing strategy.

These mindsets and principles from the previous chapter are used by leading guru investors like Warren Buffet, John Neff, and Peter Lynch, which is what makes for their investment success. Following their example, you have to ensure that you do not let your emotions get the better of you in the stock market. By doing so, you can avoid making investment mistakes and better hold an investment over the long run.

Investing is just like a game. It is full of puzzles that remain to be solved by investors.

In our opinion, investing is just like a game. It is full of puzzles that remain to be solved by investors. There are questions that investors would like to know the answers to or want to ask before committing to buying a stake in a company. We tend to look at many areas, from the company's business perspective, fundamentals, and management, to its valuation, before we commit to a buy or sell decision. When making such decisions, it is a good idea to classify these areas into simple pieces of puzzles that you would be able to put together to get a complete picture. By doing so, you are able to consolidate these areas into a simple model, as shown in Figure 3.1, to help you become successful at investing.

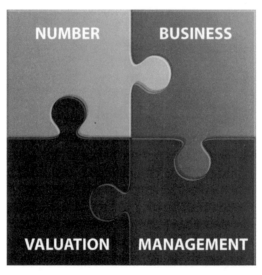

Figure 3.1   The Jigsaw Puzzle Model

The model in Figure 3.1 is one of the greatest tools that we have developed to make investing as easy as possible. We have created this model to help investors uncover a wealth of information about a company. Since humans are by nature emotional creatures, we can be inconsistent in how we assess a company. As it is, it is nearly impossible for us to completely put our emotions aside when investing. By following this model closely, you will be able to avoid herding or bringing your emotions to the stock market. This is because the Jigsaw Puzzle Model has neither emotion nor ego. Instead, it is very consistent and unbiased.

On top of this model, patience is all you need to invest successfully, after you have acquired an understanding of the business and its management, read financial statements, and determined a stock's intrinsic value. As you already know by now, it is this combination of factors that influences your investment decisions. Yardsticks, such as the price to earnings (PE) ratio and dividend yield, are insufficient for you to make a thorough investment decision. This model provides a set of criteria that you must follow closely, for all four pieces of the puzzle must fit together before you decide to purchase a particular stock. As a result, this model makes the actual decision as to when to buy and sell easier.

The Jigsaw Puzzle Model has neither emotion nor ego.

The Art and Science of Investing

Investing can be divided into two sections; it is part art and part science. Value investors emphasize pure quantitative assessment, *science*; growth investors focus on pure qualitative assessment, *art* (see Figure 3.2). Having strong fundamentals, or science, is a good start, but it only tells half the story. When it comes to investing in growth companies, you have to consider the qualitative measurement (nonnumerical assessment) in your analysis, as they are key factors in determining a company's future growth and whether it becomes a successful growth company.

Investing can be divided into two sections; it is part art and part science.

We have discussed the making of a value-growth investor and how powerful it is when we combine value and growth investing strategies. Now we will tell you that successful investing is a combination

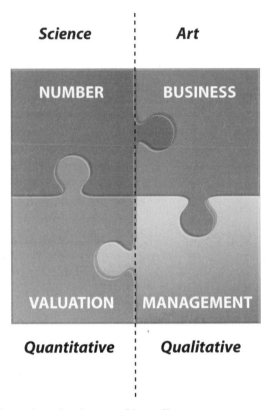

Figure 3.2   The art and science of investing

of art and science. It is an art that requires skill to find a good business within your circle of competence and assess management creditability and integrity. It is also a science that calculates the fundamentals (numerical assessment), so that you know how to value the company. For the model to work successfully, both aspects must be considered. Investors tend to give too much weight to things that can be measured, while ignoring factors that cannot be measured. This is one of the key reasons that most value investors focus too much on quantitative analysis and are caught in a value trap, through paying less attention to the art of investing. That said, finding good growth companies can be tedious and difficult. However, if you know what to look for during your research stage, you are likely to identify some potential companies in a way that is effective and efficient. And you can convert useful data into facts to support your investment decisions.

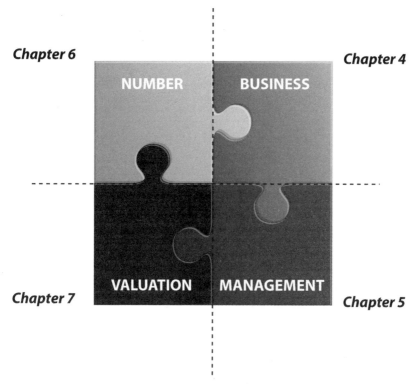

Figure 3.3   Different Pieces of the Jigsaw Puzzle Model

As shown in Figure 3.3, the model can be further divided into four pieces, where each piece delves into investment methods used by successful investors like Warren Buffett, Peter Lynch, Jim Collins, Charlie Munger, and Philip Fisher. Each piece has its own methodology that must be fulfilled before you can move on to the next piece of the puzzle. Additionally, when selecting a potential company to invest in, all four pieces of the puzzle have to come together.

In other words, you cannot have a good business with bad or dishonest managers running the company. And you can have a company with good management and business, but it yields unsatisfactory returns if you are to purchase its stocks at the wrong valuation, that is, overpaid. In which case, we are not concerned whether the market is quoting us at $1 or $1.05. Instead, we are more interested if we can buy growth companies at $0.50 with $1 worth of value and potential to grow further. Even if a company has potential

Table 3.1   Breakdown of the Jigsaw Puzzle Model

Jigsaw Pieces	Measurement	Value Growth Investor
Business	Qualitative	Yes
Management	Qualitative	Yes
Numbers	Quantitative	Yes
Valuation	Quantitative	Yes

to grow in the next 10 years—with competent and capable management, as well as undervalued—but if it is financed heavily by debt, we would avoid it. In our opinion, the risks are too high, and a company with such a profile is likely to be badly hit if a crisis strikes. However, not all debts are bad. For instance, real estate investment companies constantly have to use debt to finance the acquisition of a new property. Such is the nature of the real estate industry, where price fluctuations of a property are more moderate, compared to equity. In that case, we place more emphasis on capital preservation before capital appreciation, as the latter will take care of itself. The purpose is to avoid permanent loss of capital. In summary, Table 3.1 provides a breakdown of the Jigsaw Puzzle Model.

As mentioned earlier, you must master each of the next four chapters and put them together in order for this model to work; there is no way one chapter will teach you everything you need to make an informed decision to buy or sell.

You must learn the essence of all four pieces if you truly want to become a successful value-growth investor.

As it is, the Jigsaw Puzzle Model is like a flowchart, there to assist you, step by step, in selecting potential fast-growing companies that are likely to be winners. Since this model relies on information to support a decision, value-growth investors must know how to find the required facts from the right sources. Of course, we are not saying that by sticking to this model, you are likely to be right on every stock you pick. But, by sticking to this strategy, we believe you can pick more winning growth companies. This is our ultimate goal in sharing this model. However, before you begin to apply the model, you must know where to look for the right information.

Looking for the Right Information

Information to determine good growth companies is available to all levels of investors from a variety of sources. However, you need to be trained to look for the right information in the right places while, at the same time, ignoring all the noise in the market. Facts about a company are not actually facts if you obtain them from brokers or friends. You must go further to check whether these are reliable sources. The more reliable the source, the more accurately you will be able to decide on a company. This reliability can be accessed by browsing the Internet or doing ground checks. In the coming chapters, we will tell you exactly where to look for this information. Generally, information can be obtained from a company's announcements, or from outsiders (e.g., analysts).

Information Released by the Company

Such information is released to outside investors. In Asia, it can be commonly found on major stock exchanges like www.sgx.com (Singapore), www.bursamalaysia.com (Malaysia), www.set.or.th (Thailand), www.idx.co.id (Indonesia), www.hkex.com.hk (Hong Kong), and the company's official website, as well as financial firms that provide subscription investment services like www.shareinvestor.com. Using these sources, investors can obtain access to a wide range of information that is released to the public, including quarterly reports, annual reports, prospectuses, insider buying and selling activity, and other latest news, including press releases related to the company. Your job is to look for any significant announcements regarding the company, understand their impact, and then factor that data into your decision-making process, along with other information.

Out of all the information released, the annual report is one of the most vital sources of information by which investors are able to gain sufficient knowledge about a company's business, its management team, financial results, and so on. It is a comprehensive report on the activities and progress of a company at the end of its fiscal year. Every publicly listed company is required by law to publish this document and make it available to retail investors at the same time. Value-growth investors should read and review annual reports when they intend to invest in a company.

The following is a typical breakdown of an annual report for companies listed on the SGX:

- Financial Highlights
- CEO's Statement
- Business Review
- Board of Directors and Management
- Corporate Governance
- Independent Auditor's Report
- Financial Statements
- Notes to Financial Statements
- Statistics of Shareholding
- Proxy Form

Financial highlights can often be found in the first few pages of an annual report. This section offers a quick snapshot of the company's financial performance in the past five years. For instance, a company might report its annual figures for revenue and earnings from 2006 to 2011. Since growth companies are supposed to grow at 15% or more per annum over a few years, investors can verify that a company is indeed a growth company by calculating its growth rate under this section. We will explain how to calculate such growth rates in Chapter 7.

Under the CEO's statement, the chief executive officer (CEO) will include a letter to shareholders on the company's progress, plans for future expansion, and dividends declared. We strongly advise you to read between the lines of this letter. If it includes too much technical jargon, you should avoid this company. The company's core businesses and how it generates money will be explained under the business review. Investors should also read more about the board of directors and their management qualifications. This section often reveals other companies that the directors and management hold seats on, too. Meanwhile, the responsibility of the board of directors and management to investors can be found under corporate governance, in which details about the remuneration of the board and the number of meetings attended are clearly outlined.

Annual reports will also be audited by auditors, such as Ernst & Young, Deloitte & Touch, and others, to provide a true and fair view of the financial statements to investors. Although the auditors may give the company a clean audit, you should not take that to mean free of fraud in all instances, as auditors often rely on information provided by the management. Some signs that suggest the information might be dodgy include the engagement of small, unknown auditors or frequent change of auditors.

In an annual report, a listed company's financial statements are its main scorecard at each financial year-end. These statements provide the numbers for investors to gauge the top- to bottom-line performance of their investment.

Some signs that suggest the information might be dodgy include the engagement of small, unknown auditors or frequent change of auditors.

From the financial statement, it will be possible to compare two things:

1. The performance of the company over different financial periods (e.g., Year 2010 versus Year 2011)
2. The company's performance compared to that of other companies in the same industry (e.g., Company A versus Company B)

Many investors avoid reading these statements, as they contain many complicated numbers. However, it is really not as tough as you might think, as your job is merely to know what and where the key metrics are and take them into consideration when finding a good growth company. In doing so, it is very important to understand these key metrics, as they disclose signs (e.g., manipulation) both good and bad. In an annual report, the financial statements are comprised of the balance sheet, income statement, and cash flow statement. Companies will usually release quarterly, half yearly, or annual reports every three months, six months and every year, respectively.

The balance sheet summarizes the final balances of assets and liabilities on a specific date at the end of an accounting period—for example, quarterly, half-yearly, or annually. In layman's terms, the balance sheet shows what assets the company owns and what it owes and its net worth (equity or shareholders' funds). It offers a snapshot of a company's financial position at a specific point in time.

The income statement (or profit and loss statement) summarizes a company's financial performance over two periods (quarterly, half-yearly, annually). It tells us whether the company has been profitable during the accounting period.

The cash flow statement tracks the movement of cash inflows and outflows through operations, investments, and financing. It measures the ability of a company to generate cash through various activities. Cash flow is the lifeblood of a company's business; it is important to examine how a company converts revenue into cash and then reinvests that cash to expand the business and generate returns to shareholders. The top line of this statement is the net profit before tax (taken from the income statement), while the bottom line is the net increase or decrease in cash.

When there are surprise earnings or assets, a company will normally provide a detailed explanation under the notes to financial statement. Under statistics of shareholding, the report shows the total number of outstanding shares and the top 20 to 40 biggest shareholders in the company. This section can be very useful in understanding the percentage of ownership held by management or outside investors. Last, there is a proxy form to invite someone on an investor's behalf to attend the annual general meeting (AGM), if he or she is unable to attend. The AGM is conducted once a year for shareholders to approve important agenda items highlighted in the last few pages of the annual report to shareholders. If you own shares in the company, you are entitled to attend the AGM. This is a very important meeting; shareholders should attend as the meeting allows individual investors to question the board face to face. It is also the best chance for us to find out whether the directors are candid in answering our questions. By attending the AGM, investors are able to get a better feel for and understand a company's management.

When a company goes through an initial public offer (IPO) to raise capital for expansion, it often issues a prospectus. The prospectus outlines the company's business, finances, risks, and expansion plans for the capital raised. Investors can find a lot of information in this report.

In addition, most listed companies usually have an investor relations department, which is responsible for keeping shareholders apprised of the latest developments and key announcements, and handles queries from all shareholders. Investors are the main source of capital, and by attracting more and more investors, the company's share price will increase (in theory). Shareholders can call an investor relations officer to inquire about the business, its management, financial performance, or any other related information. If you would like to find out more, you might contact the officer-in-charge. Normally, the investor relations officer provides good answers to investors. However, while they are legally required to remain impartial, these officers may be biased toward their employer. As such, it is important to keep information dispensed by these personnel in context and never to make an investment decision solely based on the information they provide. Investors can get the contact number or email address from the company's website under investor relations. Investors can also request a hard copy of the annual report and prospectus from the investor relations officer or Google them. As we become more environmentally aware, we encourage you to download annual reports from the company's official website or respective stock exchange website.

Information from Outsiders

Outsiders refers to brokers, friends, or other retail investors who have shown interest in a particular company. For instance, analysts are paid to study and conduct research about a company's future prospects for their clients. They provide a good source of information for investors, as they have invested a substantial amount of time studying the company. However, again, investors should not follow their advice completely because it is purely an opinion based on their findings. As value-growth investors, it is also our job to do ground research similar to that of an analyst. Such research is called *scuttlebutting*, and it is a very useful strategy developed by Philip Fisher.

In his book *Common Stock and Uncommon Profits*, Philip Fisher wrote:

> The business grapevine is a remarkable thing. It is amazing what an accurate picture of the relative points of strength and weakness of each company in an industry can be obtained from a representative cross-section of the opinions of those who in one way or another are concerned with any particular company. Most people, particularly if they feel sure there is no danger of their being quoted, like to talk about the field of work in which they are engaged and will talk rather freely about their competitors. Go to five companies in an industry, ask each of them intelligent questions about the points of strength and weakness of the other four, and nine times out of ten a surprisingly detailed and accurate picture of all five will emerge.

As mentioned earlier, investment is part art, part science. There is a side to it that is art, such as finding information not released by the company. To do this, investors have to go the extra mile to find information that might provide great investment insights. To do so, you could go down to do an in-person check on the daily operations of a company on your radar. While this takes time and effort, it allows you to make a more informed investment decision.

Scuttle-butting is often useful when it comes to assessing the qualitative side. Websites like www.socialmention .com, www.seekingalpha.com, and www.research.ly serve as good platforms for investors to know what has recently been mentioned about a company in social media. Investors can perform a simple search by keying in the product's name, company's name, or the name of the management under the search tab to see what others are saying about a company. In addition, some forums have discussion areas that talk all about listed stocks (e.g., www .valuebuddies.com in Singapore), focusing on both the quantitative and qualitative sides. On top of the content in such forums, do a search to see what comes up. You will be surprised at how much a company has been discussed. If you have friends investing in the same company, it does not hurt to ask them on their views of the company and why they invest in it. In the upcoming chapters, we will show you what to look out for and what questions to ask.

During an AGM, it also pays to talk to other prospective investors that have a common interest in the company; they may be more than willing to share their information. Understandably, these are places to gather more resources. After the formal AGM, refreshments are usually served to investors. This presents another great chance for investors to talk to the board of directors privately.

In conclusion, value-growth investors do not necessarily need expensive services to find a good growth company. With so much information available elsewhere at almost no cost, it is not difficult for you to identify quality stocks to include in your portfolio and start enjoying the benefits of compounding your hard-earned money.

Summary

- Quantitative measurement (numerical assessment) includes everything from simple financial ratios, such as return on equity, to more complicated analysis, such as discounted earnings models to determine the future value. It can be measured—science.

- Qualitative measurement (nonnumerical assessment) includes understanding the business model, its sustainability and ability to grow further in the future, while at the same time giving investors what they need to know about its management and their track records. It cannot be measured—art.

- Read historical annual reports (up to five years) to get a better insight into a company's business, management, and past financial performance. In addition, read the company's prospectus to get a better understanding of business risks and expansion plans. Make full use of technology platforms to gather valuable information online.

- Attend AGMs to interact with the board of directors and fellow investors.

CHAPTER 4

Business—The First Piece of the Puzzle

Understand a Company's Business Model

The very first piece of the Jigsaw Puzzle Model is business. It is placed before all the other pieces because of its importance. Purchasing shares in a listed company is the equivalent of buying a piece of the company. Therefore, by purchasing a company's equities, an investor becomes part owner. Warren Buffett once said: "I am a better businessman because I am an investor; I am a better investor because I am a businessman." He meant that, in order to become a good investor, you must think and act like a business owner when you own a particular stock. Whatever affects the company's business or fundamentals affects the value of your holdings in that particular company. In other words, if you want to outperform the market, you have to understand the business you are buying. Knowing the business model inside out should provide investors some level of certainty and reduces the risk when purchasing the stock. Furthermore, it should provide the investor an edge over the others (who do not understand the company's business model) to see where the business will be in the future, who are the direct or indirect competitors, and the likelihood of the company succeeding.

Fundamentally, you must understand the inputs used to produce final products or services sold to consumers. Look at the largest products or services contributing to the revenue and earnings of a business segment and determine how and where they are derived. Is the customer largely a single or concentrated customer base? On top of answering this question, you also need to know which markets the company is serving geographically, be it locally or internationally, as well as how big its market share is, based on its core businesses and the consumer profile (e.g., high or low end).

Refer to Figure 4.1; you should also know where the invested capital is directed and how it is returned to shareholders in the form of profits. Although investing in stocks gives you the benefits of ownership without the headaches, knowing why you buy a stock gives you more confidence to hold the company in the long run and make key investment decisions.

For instance, you may have decided to buy Creative Technology at S$8 per share in 2007 because you thought it was cheap and a good deal, as it dropped from its high price of S$25 in 2005. But, because the company has been operating in the highly competitive technology sector, we feel there is a need to scuttle-butt to determine if a bottom is forming or is there no end in sight. As it is, with Creative Technology shops closing down due to losing market share to competitors, the company does not seem to display much in the way of prospects. At the time of writing this book, the share price continued to drop from S$8 to S$3 even when the market had recovered from Euro debt crisis.

In this case, understanding the business and its competitive advantages will enable you to recognize your losses early. At this

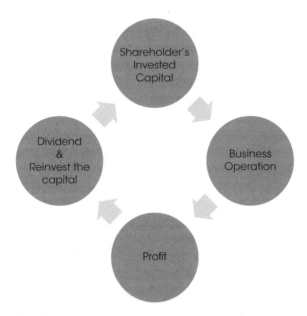

Figure 4.1 Capital flow in a company

point, note that if you can be six months ahead of the market, you should make money or, at the very least, avoid losing money. And this is one of the strategies when picking up good growth companies. In essence, understanding a business can be thought of in two ways: it could be a simple business, or it can be a company that falls within your circle of competence.

Simple Business

Simple businesses are easy to understand and evaluate and have financial statements that are straightforward; nearly anyone can understand them. Investors will quickly understand how these companies make money and where the money comes from.

Examples of companies with simple businesses:

- Malaysia:
  - Hartalega Sdn Bhd—They sell examination gloves
  - Dutch Lady Milk Industries Bhd—They sell milk
- Singapore:
  - Singapore Press Holdings (SPH) Ltd—They sell newspapers and magazines

- ◆ VICOM Ltd—They service cars
- ◆ Super Group Ltd—They sell instant coffee
- Indonesia:
  - ◆ PT Multi-Bintang Indonesia Tbk.—They sell beer
  - ◆ Ace Hardware Indonesia Tbk.—They sell hardware
- Hong Kong:
  - ◆ Want Want China Holdings Ltd—They sell snack foods

Simple businesses are not necessarily businesses that will do well and prosper. Understandably, all these companies have their share of ups and downs. However, you have to admit that these companies are easier to understand than offshore and shipping companies. Thus, when someone asks you to invest in a company that you have never heard of, the better way to understand it is to ask them what business the company is in. If you can easily understand the explanation, you can conclude that it is a simple business. Otherwise, it is better to study it further or simply avoid it altogether. You can test whether you have understood the business well by putting it into words that a 10-year-old child or an 80-year-old granny can understand. While this may sound ridiculous, it is certainly a good way to gauge your understanding of the company's business. For instance, the food and beverage (F&B) industry comprises companies operating under a simple business model and, of course, are on the lips of investors, as all of us take an interest in food, regardless of market conditions. Needless to say, there are many F&B companies listed on the Singapore Exchange (SGX). It is then your job to identify the good ones from the bad ones by studying them carefully.

The concept of simplicity—simple and understandable— is often misunderstood by the average investor. The confusion is perhaps due to the fact that it is so simple! For instance, Nokia has an easy-to-understand business because it sells phones to consumers. Akira manufactures and sells electronics to consumers, so their business is easy to understand and articulate as well. Problems occur when people confuse familiarity with simplicity. Being familiar with some products and how they make money does not guarantee that the company will continue to make more money in future. You might be familiar with Sembawang Music Stores, which are seen in Singapore shopping malls. Investors might assume that the company has a simple business model, as they simply sell audio and movies to consumers. But, in late 2009, the company filed for bankruptcy due to poor business, as a result of changing trends among consumers. Consumers had started to move from electronic content to digital content, where music and movies could be easily downloaded from the Internet at cheaper prices.

By our definition, a simple business is an easy-to-understand business that should not experience major changes—be it 10 or 20 years later. For example, people will not stop visiting dentists 10 years down the road. They will not stop drinking beer 20 years later. They will still send their cars for inspection when required. Thus, companies that offer these products and services are deemed simple businesses that do not suffer major changes, compared to a company like TT International, which sells Akira consumer electronic equipment. In their case, they must stay innovative and constantly upgrade their products, lest being ousted by competitors. Other technology companies, like Nokia, also do not fit the bill of being a simple business.

In relation to this point, the bottom line is to avoid investing in technology stocks unless you have been working in the technology industry for years. If you do avoid such companies, your

> *A simple business is an easy-to-understand business that should not experience major changes—be it 10 or 20 years later.*

risks will be significantly reduced. Having said that, you might miss spectacular returns on your portfolio, but nevertheless, you will avoid investing in something beyond your understanding. This will lead us to the next point of circle of competence.

Circle of Competence

Some businesses are not easy to understand by the average person, but you may understand them thoroughly. This type of business may be within your capacity due to your years of experience in it. Such businesses are then said to be within your circle of competence. This term was coined by Warren Buffett when he said, "You don't have to be an expert on every company, or even many. You only have to be able to evaluate companies within your circle of competence. The size of that circle is not very important; knowing its boundaries, however, is vital."

For example, as an engineer, you have an edge in investing in the engineering industry. A company such as ST Engineering Ltd is within your circle of competence. If you are in the health-care industry, a company like Thomson Medical Centre is within your circle of competence. In this case, you understand the company better than others. Better still, you have access to insider information.

> You don't have to be an expert on every company, or even many. You only have to be able to evaluate companies within your circle of competence. The size of that circle is not very important; knowing its boundaries, however, is vital.
>
> —*Warren Buffet*

Others that are not related to work could be products or services that you use in your daily life, which might include products that you use when you wake up, such as toothpaste and razors, or trains that bring you to your workplace, or the Internet that keeps you connected with friends. This could also be the newspaper that you subscribe to with Singapore Press Holding, or the products and services you pay for every day or month. This could also be the food courts, like Food Republic, where you head for lunch. Or think about your shopping habits. Perhaps you often head to Cold Storage or even 7-Eleven to get some snacks for yourself. If you feel like getting a luxury watch for yourself, you might go to The Hour Glass or Hengdeli to take a look. When you need a wisdom tooth extracted, you may go to Q&M Dental for screening. At night, you may want to party and grab drinks manufactured by F&N. And what are you wearing right now? It could be clothes from Adidas or TopShop (under Wingtai Asia) or Padini. When you are traveling, which airline do you travel with? Is it Singapore Airlines (SIA) or Airasia? As you might have guessed, some of these companies are listed on the SGX, while others are listed on HKE or Bursa Malaysia. As an investor, it is your job to find out more about these companies and determine how profitable they are.

That is not the end. You will also need to dig out more information to assess whether they are truly growth companies in the next 10 to 20 years from now. Needless to say, we do not advise you to buy shares in a company just because you use their products frequently. After all, some of these companies are simply so big that growing at a rate of more than 15 percent per annum would be difficult to accomplish. Nevertheless, you have every reason to be interested in the company, especially after you have carried out your research.

The key thing is that value-growth investors should not stray too far outside their circle of competence. In other words, a dentist should not invest in the oil and gas industry, since it is not within his circle of competence. An F&B store manager should not invest in shipping industry (unless she knows something about it). Going by this rule, we do not invest in oil companies because we do not know how to value an oil services firm. Instead, we leave it to someone who is competent in that field rather than subject ourselves to risk.

Furthermore, some industries require an enormous amount of time to study before you can become competent to invest in them. Again, you may be familiar with certain banks (e.g., UOB, OCBC, Maybank, Public Bank) and are maybe even a regular customer. But if you do not understand the banking industry, you should stay away. It can be difficult to understand their business model unless you work in that industry or have insight into it. Banks may have large, complex derivative exposures and carry with them certain risks. This can make it difficult to estimate the profitability of the business.

Going Beyond the Limit

Of course, you can research any area outside your circle of competence. There comes a point when you realize that there is a limit to the number of companies you can invest in. This is the point at which you have to start to increase your circle of competence or area of understanding. For instance, if you know the demand for healthcare products is going to boom in the future, as a result of growing affluence among developing countries (i.e., China), you may want to learn more about this industry. Indeed, it is a good idea to do your homework before going into any new industry. As a successful value-growth investor, you should be constantly learning and stretching your knowledge outside your circle of competence. But, before you expand your circle too wide, make sure your initial circle of competence is fully understood. Otherwise, simply stick to what you already understand.

To make this selection easier, you could follow Charlie Munger's or Jim Collins's method of selecting companies based on your circle of competence or businesses that are not only easy to understand but also seemingly boring.

Charlie Munger's Method

There are three baskets Munger commonly uses in his method, namely: in, out, and too tough to understand. To identify potential yes candidates, you look for an easy-to-understand and seemingly boring business, or one that is inside your circle of competence. In other words, if you know something about the company and it is in your circle of competence, you already have the edge. Few companies will survive this process. For one, technology companies will go right to the too-tough-to-understand basket. IPO companies will immediately go to the no basket. In relation to this, it is possible for you to understand some IPO companies that fall within your circle of competence but do not have a sufficient track record, making it very dangerous to invest with them. And for those companies that have been given a yes, screening will then move on to assessing the sustainability of the business as well as other considerations. The process is that simple and efficient (see Figure 4.2).

Figure 4.2   Three Baskets in Charlie Munger's Method

Source: Peter D. Kaufman, *Poor Charlie's Almanack: The Wit and Wisdom of Charles T. Munger.*

Jim Collins's Method

Jim Collins created a model called the Three Circles to let people find businesses they already know and understand better than others. The Three Circles consist of passion, talent, and money, as shown in Figure 4.3.

In the first circle, passion, write down all the things that you love to do, things that you are willing to sacrifice your time to do. In the second circle, talent, write down all the things that you are really good at, be it work, sports, or something else. In the last circle, money, write down where you spend or earn your money. After you have stated all these in the three circles, see if something appears in more than one circle. This is an area in which you probably have a much better understanding of than others. With the help of these three circles, you can start searching in the industry sector for businesses or products relating to the word that appears in more than one circle. In other words, this is within your circle of competence.

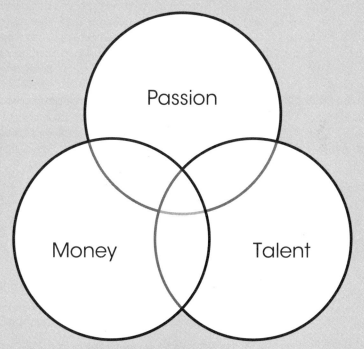

Figure 4.3   The Three Circles

Source: Jim Collins, Good to Great: Why Some Companies Make the Leap . . . and Others Don't (New York: HarperCollins, 2001).

Competitive Advantage

Back in the 2000s, people queued patiently just to purchase a cup of bubble tea. At that time, when the first bubble-tea shop, Quickly, opened, everyone was crazy about it. Even though each cup of bubble tea cost S$3 to S$5, people were willing to pay the price. It was one of the most profitable bubble-tea businesses in Singapore. Thereafter, others responded to the demand for bubble tea, and many rival chains were set up. Soon bubble-tea shops were everywhere in Singapore, from the interchange to shopping centers. As supply increased, the price of bubble tea dropped to S$1.50 per cup. After two years of the bubble-tea craze, demand started to decrease sharply and bubble tea shops started to fold.

Quickly was the first shop to start the trend and the first shop to fold. This goes to show that Quickly's business did not have a competitive advantage, as it was easy for competitors to penetrate into their market and seize their market share. Here, bubble tea is one good example of a business with a product that did not have a competitive advantage, thereby undermining the business profits. For example, investors tend to look at companies that have grown profits in the past few years and assume the trend will continue in future.

In the world of investments, we cannot simply rely on a series of past growth earning rates alone and assume that they will continue to produce the same profit year after year. If investing were that simple, we would have been richer just by investing in companies that behave this way. And this book would be thinner. Value-growth investors do not rely solely on the history of a company. Instead, we find the company's ability to sustain its profit in the long run as well as its ability to grow. Finding a company's competitive advantage is crucial to knowing whether the company will be able to sustain its profitability (see Figure 4.4).

Competitive advantage is defined as the ability of the company to sustain its business and keep its competitors at bay, thereby protecting long-term profits and market share. In other words, a company is able to provide a good or service similar to competitors while simultaneously outperforming them in profit generation or by being the only player in the field (monopoly). This is commonly known as having an *economic moat*. These companies tend to have superior returns in the long run because they are able to

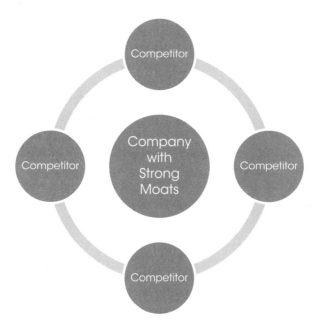

Figure 4.4   Companies with a competitive advantage are better able to keep competitors at bay

command a premium price for their products or services. Besides keeping peers under pressure, these companies tend to outperform the overall market index over time. When it comes to investing, competitive advantage must be factored into the value of a company. Good growth companies must have a competitive advantage; their core businesses should not be easily replicated by competitors or should be replicated only with great difficulty. This creates a high barrier to entry. Examples of moats are strong brands, monopolies, lowest-cost producers, exclusive licenses, repetition, and convenience. Therefore, they deserve higher premium valuations relative to a mediocre company.

Naturally, a strong brand is important, as it portrays everything good and valuable about the company. Fred Perry, for example, manages to convince teenagers to pay more for a T-shirt just because it has a logo printed on it. The same goes

Competitive advantage *is defined as the ability of the company to sustain its business and keep its competitors at bay, thereby protecting long-term profits and market share.*

for brands like Louis Vuitton and Coach. These brands have built a reputation among their customers for quality products and services. Furthermore, brands can have a strong impact on the consumer mind-set. When we think of eating ramen, Ajisen comes to mind. When we think of drinking chicken soup, Brand's Essence of Chicken will be our choice. When we want to buy bread for breakfast, BreadTalk often speaks to us. When we think of drinking a cup of iced Milo, Nestlé lingers in our mind. This is known as *brand association.*

When a company has control of the entire market, it is said to have monopolized the market. For instance, SPH is a monopoly in the newspaper and magazine market in Singapore. It has no problem increasing advertising fees or publication prices, provided the economy is not in a recession. CerebosPac, a producer of Brand's, has an Essence of Chicken market share of more than 80 percent. VICOM, a vehicle inspection company, has a market share of more than 80 percent. These companies, as market leaders, should be able to increase prices on their products and services without affecting volume sales materially. Most likely, their smaller rivals will follow suit as price takers, keeping the pie proportionate. Another example would be the SGX, where nearly every investor will have to pass if they need to trade public shares in Singapore's stock market. As monopolies in the market, these companies are able to exercise what are also known as *toll-gate effects.*

Location—Consumers seek to obtain products or services that are convenient and easily accessible. Thus, location is one of the most important factors, when products or services must be easily accessible to customers. Look at Q&M Dental Health Care, for example, which has stores near MRT stations and in neighborhoods all across Singapore. As they are located at high-population traffic areas, it allows ease of access to consumers who can head out to a nearby outlet to engage dental services.

Repetition/Recurring—Products that are used often and wear out fast have to be bought again and again. These products should be readily available in the local supermarket (e.g., Super Instant Coffee Mix, Gardenia Bread). A visit to 7-Eleven stores will help you discover many such products.

Sometimes a company can come up with numerous moats protecting them. Hartalega, a medical glove manufacturer in Malaysia, has positioned itself as one of the lowest-cost producers in its industry, benefiting from its cutting-edge technology. Aside from being a lowest-cost producer, Hartalega is also in a highly recurring business, in which the majority of clients are operating in highly regulated environments, such as the healthcare sector. Thus, hygiene cannot be compromised, and gloves may only be used once. Once the gloves are used up, clients need to repurchase gloves from Hartalage.

Now, if a company possesses one or more of these attributes, you have a better reason to invest in the company in the long run. Most important, it must have a competitive advantage to stay ahead of its rivals and any newcomers. One of the easiest ways to gauge whether a company has a competitive advantage is from its margin. By comparing its margin with its competitors, it is easy to tell which company (within the same industry) has better profitability.

Knowing the Competitors

To confirm whether a company has competitive advantages working in its favor, you have to find out who its competitors are. Here we are interested in growth companies that make a greater profit than their competitors. To determine this, you need to read the annual reports of their competitors. This will help you discover how well the company is competing against its rivals. For instance, CerebosPac—Brand's Essence of Chicken—has competitors such as Eu Yan Sang and New Moon. By quickly going through their annual and analyst reports, we learned that Cerebos is still the market leader in terms of chicken essence products, with over 80 percent of the market share.

Moving forward, you will understand the important things to look out for, based on our model. Things like comparing profit margins and market share are the main priorities. Reading industry reports and researching on competitors are also good ways to get a handle on the competitive landscape.

A good way to find competitors is through analysts' reports. However, do not rely on their recommendations, just use their data to help make an informed decision. In such reports, analysts often highlight a company and compare it with other companies within the same industry. However, if the company is already within your circle of competence, you are likely to know who its competitors are.

When attending the AGM of a company, it helps to ask the board this question: "Why should customers do business with you and not your competitors?" This question can prove very insightful in helping you find the competitive advantage of the company in terms of price, service, and unique strategy. Competitors can be a good source of information. By getting answers from them, the leader will become evident.

Think Like a Customer through the Scuttle-Butting Process

The success of a business is highly dependent on customers' preferences. Sam Walton, founder of Walmart, once said, "There is only one boss—the customer. And he can fire everybody in the company, including the chairman, simply by spending his money somewhere else." Hence, knowing what customers need and want is very important as a businessman and investor. You must think as though you are a customer who will do business with the company.

Test its service or product at the point of sales. By doing so, you want to know how the company treats its customers. In this case, the reason for scuttle-butting is because many companies like Walmart and McDonald's have won their customers' hearts through high-quality service. You simply cannot experience the quality of the service provided by McDonald's by reading an annual report or calling its investor relations personnel; you have to go in person to test its product and services.

We are also better off knowing whether a company is in deep trouble before other analysts or experts get wind of it. Simply put, visit a store that is listed on the stock exchange. For example, a shop might have been bustling with customers when you stepped into it in a particular year but a lot quieter when you visited it again a year later. If you had been observant, you would have guessed that sales would be affected even before the company announced it in its annual report to the investors. So prior to the announcement, the company was still trading at its high as everyone was bullish about its future expansion. But by doing a site visit, you would have known otherwise.

You simply cannot experience the quality of the service provided by McDonald's by reading an annual report or calling its investor relations personnel; you have to go in person to test its product and services.

Scuttle-butting provides a strong, empirically based indicator, but it is limited to brick-and-mortar businesses. For instance, when we scuttle-butt Japan Food's restaurants, we would notice that the restaurants are usually packed at dinnertime, and when compared to its competitors, you would realize that Japan Food's restaurants are busier than the rest. This gives us a good indication of its performance and the advantages that the company has in the market. When we went to Indonesia on vacation, and visited sub-franchise Ajisen outlets in major shopping malls in the suburbs, we discovered, to our surprise, that the restaurants were packed even after the peak period, which is a strong indication that the business model works well even in overseas markets. Expansion, in terms of volume, would not likely be a major issue if management intends to open or sub-franchise more outlets in Indonesia. In our opinion, this company has scalability power.

We repeated this process with Soup Restaurant, a Chinese F&B restaurant. In this case, we visited one of the outlets around Seah Street in Singapore and spoke to the restaurant manager about company's operations.

To know a company's future direction, we need to identify potential drivers that can continue to generate sales and, in turn, earnings growth.

Our understanding of the business operation got better after the visits. On the same holiday trip to Indonesia, we visited Dian Xiao Er, one of Soup Restaurant's subsidiaries there. The outlet seemed to be empty, while other restaurants, such as Japan Food, were packed during lunch hour. This scuttlebutting process tells us that Japan Food is a scalable process in other countries, be it in a Muslim or Chinese market. It is more capable of attracting and retaining customers. As for Soup Restaurant, its food appeals only to the Chinese market. So if you have done the scuttle-butting process, you would have chosen Japan Food over Soup Restaurant, in terms of the success of its growth expansion plan, where our only concern with the latter was its expansion plans in overseas markets. In this case, we found that the sustainability and growth of Soup Restaurant is mainly dependent on a single market in Singapore (where the majority of their outlets are in operation). But, to be a great growth company, the company really must be able to expand into the overseas market as well.

To know a company's future direction, we need to identify potential drivers that can continue to generate sales and, in turn, earnings growth. To do so, we do not predict but make estimates based on a company's extent of success in terms of expansion plans, while retaining its existing customer base. By doing so, we ensure certainty in our investments before we know how much a company will be worth in future.

Finding Future Growth Drivers

There are few ways that companies can achieve high growth in the future: sell more products and services or venture into overseas markets. Here the most common source in uncovering potential growth drivers is in the annual report. Through the annual report, you can gain an overview of the company's core business, understand how it makes money and what the growth drivers are in keeping the business growing for the past few years. An understanding of a company's history may reveal its growth strategy or consistency with success and failure. It would also reveal future expansion plans. For instance, Q&M has a lot of room for growth in Singapore and China. The group's target is to own and operate 60 clinics in Singapore by 2015. In China, the group intends to have 50 clinics and some laboratories, which is a key growth driver. Investors must remember to look out for signs that the expansion plan is not working well by visiting the new outlets. Once you know the company is growing to its limit, you must act accordingly. In which case, it will be too late if you wait for your broker to inform you that the company's latest results are rather disappointing. To stay ahead of others, check a company's expansion plan to determine whether it is likely to grow or slow down. At this point, you should investigate whether the company has overseas expansion plans. Scuttle-butting, will not only give you an edge over other financial experts but will also allow you to find potential future growth companies. For instance, when you are out shopping, something that you have found to sell well is a sure sign of growing sales. Learn to identify these trends early and seek out opportunities to enter at the right price before the market notices them. This is the secret to making big bucks when investing in growth companies that are not yet unearthed. If you are already reading about high sales growth in a company, it is probably too late.

Other than business-to-consumer companies, not all companies provide services to consumers that can be verified via scuttle- butting.

For example, a company like SIA Engineering—a business-to-business company—provides engineering services to SIA planes. You would not be able to easily determine whether there is any potential growth unless you worked in the industry, talked to the company's suppliers, management, or staffs. For such companies, we have to find other key factors, like demographics, and their ability to expand into other overseas markets.

Large-scale demographic trends should provide us with a good hint of the direction in which the company is heading. Today, we are especially interested in age, population

> *When a business is thought to have future growth potential, it does not mean that the company will definitely prosper.*

centers, and international politics. Psychographics, such as lifestyle and buying habits, cannot be ignored. We know the population is aging, but it is also wealthier than in previous generations. Common sense suggests that aging populations in wealthy countries will create a windfall for healthcare companies. Thanks to advances in nutrition and hygiene, people are generally healthier, and are also more obsessed with their quality of life and will spend money freely for more energy, vitality, and health. This provides a good opportunity for the healthcare industry to boom and do well in the long run. Likewise, oil and gas companies sell a scarce resource to energy-hungry, growing populations with high consumption and demand. In developing countries, such as China, India, Indonesia, and Russia, the demand will be even higher. As middle- and working-class citizens in developing countries get better jobs, they will earn higher salaries, which will spur them to spend more. With higher incomes, they will spend not only on basic necessities but also on luxury items. However, products or services that work well in the developed world do not necessarily translate to success in the developing world. For instance, smaller and less expensive cigarette pack sizes, which sell in pieces, are effective in developing countries, as they are more affordable as compared to big cigarette packs that are deemed more popular in developed countries. As such, products have to be reformulated to appeal to this market. Also, Chinese food, when marketed in a country like Indonesia, might not work well unless it is targeted at Chinese locals, since there is a higher Muslim population in Indonesia.

When a business is thought to have future growth potential, it does not mean that the company will definitely prosper. Rather, this indicator helps us narrow down the field to see whether the target is a growth company based on key drivers of the business. We will still need to evaluate the risks involved to avoid being overly confident of a company's growth. In which case, understanding such risks is very important since growth companies are highly unstable.

Understanding Risks—What Can Go Wrong?

We will still need to evaluate the risks involved to avoid being overly confident of a company's growth.

It is important for you as an investor to not get overconfident in investing. The main reason for the failure of a growth company is not due to shrinking demand for its products but the inability to perform the many tasks required to sustain its rapid expansion. When companies go through the fast-growing stage, it may result in the following problems:

1. Poor product quality
2. Missed deadlines
3. Lower customer satisfactory
4. Management's inability to cope with the strong growth
5. Steep competition in the existing market

You must understand the risks, as these factors will affect future earnings. For you to understand the risks involved in the company you are about to invest in, you might start by reading the prospectus. This is given to shareholders when the company goes listed. Often these resources can be difficult to find, especially if the company has been around for a long time. In that case, you can search for the prospectus on the exchange's website, obtain it from the company's investor relations officer, or try searching for it on Google or other search engines. There are other risks not highlighted in the prospectus. As such, you have to uncover those risks and not rely solely on the prospectus alone. During the AGM, investors can ask these questions to help access a company's risk. One such question could be "What are the current biggest threats to your company and sector?" This question, if answered truthfully, can highlight new risks discovered by the management after its IPO.

Analysts' reports also provide good assessment of risks. They often use a SWOT (Strength, Weaknesses, Opportunities, and Threats) analysis approach when accessing a company. Here, threats and weaknesses highlight the company's potential risks. Understanding the risks will help us to achieve our long-term goals faster, because we will be fully prepared when such threats occur. In any case, the best way to reduce our risks is to have a margin of safety. This will help protect us from our downside.

By now, you should be convinced that investing in a company without understanding it may lead to disastrous consequences. Doing so will be considered speculative no matter how cheaply you bought the stock. This piece of the puzzle offers one of the hidden clues to finding good growth companies. With that, let us move on to the next piece of the puzzle—management.

Summary

- Understand the business model thoroughly, from its raw materials to the final products and/or services used by customers.
- Look out for simple and easy-to-understand businesses or businesses within your circle of competence.
- A good business with strong moats will protect earning power and keep competitors at bay.
- Periodically visit the company to assess its business conditions. A growth plan is a must in order to keep the company growing.
- Read the demographics of a country in which the company intends to expand and the products or services that it will likely benefit from.
- Understanding the risks will help you make better decisions during a crisis.

CHAPTER 5

Management—The Second Piece of the Puzzle

Management Forms the Cornerstone of a Business

The second piece of the jigsaw puzzle is management. By placing money in the stock market, we are indirectly hoping to leverage someone else's talent to compound our wealth, with that person running the business effectively in our place. The future growth of a company is highly dependent on its management. They are the board of directors, including the chief executive officer (CEO), executive or nonexecutive and independent directors, as well as senior management teams at the division level.

Having a great business in place is a good start. Good businesses produce great results in the long run; this often comes from having a great management at the helm of a company. However, many investors wrongly assume that management will take great care of their shares just because they have generated solid profits in the past. Thus, they fully trust management's capability and skip this assessment altogether. This is quite risky!

As shareholders, we view management as our working partner. As we are not in a position to run the business, we entrust the management to hire quality people to undertake the various operating functions and run the company on our behalf.

In general, a great business can normally be attributed to a great management in place. Some businesses, owing to lax management, become susceptible to acts of fraud and dishonesty. If you choose incompetent and dishonest management to run the business, you will not be able to sleep soundly at night. However, if you know that the management team is competent and honest, you are more assured of the company's operations.

A shareholder-oriented management maximizes the returns of shareholders. Such a management team should be trustworthy, candid in reporting, aligned with shareholders' interests, and have strong track records. When we assess the quality of the management, we are reducing our investment risks.

However, it is difficult for an outsider to determine if a management team is good. Nonetheless, we should never ignore assessing the management team when it comes to valuing a company, especially in relation to the track record of the management team. Here the difficulty could be a lack of knowledge as to how to assess the team, yet investors have to know who is steering the company. This is the hardest part in investing, as it requires some form of courage, commitment, and time to meet the management face to face during the annual general meeting (AGM) or during a visit to the company's headquarters. A quick tip to get to the AGM is to buy a share from the odd-lot market, which usually costs less, as compared to buying 100 or more shares.

Now let us go through the criteria to determine if a management team is sound and will work for us. Some of the telltale signs can be easily found in the annual report or news made available to investors, while others are not so obvious.

Criterion 1: Trustworthiness

Warren Buffett once said, "After some mistakes, I learned to go into business only with people whom I like, trust, and admire." He further added, "We do not wish to join with managers who lack admirable qualities, no matter how attractive the prospects of their business. We've never succeeded in making a good deal with a bad person."

This is precisely the point we want to highlight. Here, what Buffett wants is a manager who behaves responsibly and runs the company as if he or she is the owner of the company. It comes from the person's passion to achieve big goals and share a common vision with shareholders. We can only trust managers when they are able to run the business truthfully and diligently. Preferably, the management team treats the business as theirs, instead of acting like people who are hired and paid a fixed compensation.

> *One way to ascertain management's commitment is to gauge the percentage of ownership that individual managers have in a company.*

One way to ascertain management's commitment is to gauge the percentage of ownership that individual managers have in a company. As long as the ownership of the top management is substantial, they are more likely to treat the business seriously. While this does not guarantee that management will run the company diligently, it assures you that they are looking out for your best interests because part of your wealth is tied up in the same basket as theirs. With that, we can expect them to have the vision to grow their shares as much as we would as shareholders. In fact, they will do whatever it takes to grow the company. And, when the company makes money, management will be rewarded through their ownership as shareholders, with either dividends or capital appreciation.

The percentage of substantial shareholders can often be found in the annual report under statistics of shareholding. In that case, find out if the top management is rewarded with equity-linked compensation (i.e., share options, restricted stocks). For instance, in 2010, Takahashi Kenichi, CEO of Japan Food Hlds Ltd, owned 77.45 percent of total shares in the company, as seen in Table 5.1. With high ownership of shares, the chances are very high that he will work hard and drive the earnings in the long run. This is likely to translate into higher dividends, which will reward him as well as other minority shareholders.

On the other hand, heavy ownership does not by itself guarantee that a management is trustworthy. If top management sells their stakes too quickly, you must investigate further. It is preferable that they hold shares in the long run rather than buy and sell their shares frequently. As we are not traders, we do not want managers to have a trader's mindset either. Directors with little or no ownership stake are more interested in taking profits from the company rather than adding value to shareholders.

Alternatively, you can assess a management team through the compensation packages they receive. Are they overcompensating themselves, even when they are already holding a lot of shares? As CEO of Berkshire Hathaway, Buffett was paid USD100,000 in 2008. In that year, he helped the company generate a multibillion-dollar net profit. As the CEO of Apple, Steve Jobs was paid only USD1 per year, even though the company made billions of dollars in profit. In relation to this, many people are curious as to how Steve Jobs survived on just USD1 per year. The answer lies in his share ownership of the company in 1997. Through the years, Steve Jobs did not sell a single of his 5.5 million shares in Apple, even though his

Table 5.1   Shareholding in Japan Food Holding

No.	Name	No. of Shares	%
1.	Takahashi Kenichi	68,286,000	77.45
2.	HSBC (Singapore) Nominees Pte Ltd	4,000,000	4.54
3.	Sirius Venture Consulting Pte Ltd	3,981,000	4.52
4.	Loh Yih	2,973,000	3.37
5.	Shigemitsu Katsuaki	1,867,000	2.12
6.	Shigemitsu Industry Co. Ltd	1,867,000	2.12
7.	Tan Kay Toh or Yu Hea Ryeong	1,033,000	1.17
8.	DBS Vickers Securities (S) Pte Ltd	655,000	0.75
9.	Long Shing Yuan	253,000	0.29
10.	Lim Mei Chen	180,000	0.20

Source: Japan Food Holding's Annual Report 2010

holding was worth USD1.1 billion. As such, he was entitled income from dividends that were declared by Apple. So, the next question is, does it make sense to you that a CEO gets paid lavishly when the company is losing money? From an investor's point of view, it is obvious that a highly compensated CEO only thinks for himself and not what is best for the shareholders. In other words, such CEOs are taking shareholders' money and paying themselves with it.

Here is an example of someone who is shareholder-oriented: Hsu Chih-Chien, chairman of Courage Marine, did not receive any salary or incentive during the financial crisis of 2008–09. When we went to the AGM and asked him why he did not take any salary, he responded, "Why should I receive any salary when the company is going through a tough time?" Immediately, every shareholder in the meeting stood up and applauded him. Now, this is the type of management that you know you will be able to entrust with your hard-earned money. Such a management values you as a shareholder and is serious about creating more value for your investment.

Therefore, we would prefer a CEO who is able to generate $50 million in sales and $10 million in net profits to pay herself $1 million than a CEO who is able to generate the same amount of sales, incur losses for shareholders, but still pay herself $1 million because that is the market rate for a CEO.

Here the general rule is to compare net profits to salary. There is no hard rule, but a good benchmark will be to compare the company with peers in a similar industry who have the same market capitalization or consistency based on past records. Some management might claim to have generated $500 million in sales and a net profit of only $5 million yet pay themselves $10 million. In doing so, they are in fact taking investors' money out of the company to give to themselves. We do not mind that a large compensation package is paid to the board of directors, so long as they are able to run the company well. We expect leaders to be rewarded for outstanding long-term performance. In other words, we want to pay them for their able, trustworthy, and owner-oriented mindset, which helps generates profits for shareholders, preferably in the form of profit sharing. Management should be rewarded more when the company makes more money and vice versa. This can be traced through profit-sharing bonuses.

For instance, if you refer to Table 5.2, you will see that the CEO of Design Studio, Bernard Lim Leng Foo, received a remuneration that was 70 percent performance based. Meanwhile, the majority of the management team was paid based on profit sharing than a fixed salary, which acts as a reward to them for bringing the company to new heights. So, when the company makes money, they get paid more, and vice versa. Their pay should rise and fall based on the performance of the company rather than on a high fixed salary. Likewise, a company with good corporate governance is more likely to lower the salary of all employees, including its board of directors and directors' fees. (Note: From a cost perspective, it is better to have a higher variable cost structure than fixed, as it is easier to make adjustments during tough times.)

Criterion 2: Candid in Reporting

Management must have excellent communication with shareholders and a clean annual report that is easy to understand. When it comes to reporting, mistakes should be reported as transparently as possible. Growth companies are more likely to run into unexpected

Table 5.2   Remuneration band of Design Studio's directors

Remuneration Bands Name of Directors	Salary (%)	Bonus (%)	Profit Sharing (%)	Director Fees (%)	Other Benefits (%)
≥SGD1,250,000 Executive Chairman & CEO Bernard Lim Leng Foo	27	7	63	–	3
≥SGD750,000 to SSGD1,000,000 Executive Director Elin Wong Hong Keow	30	8	61	–	1
≥SGD500,000 to SGD750,000 Executive Director Kelly Ng Chai Choey	30	8	60	–	2
Executive Officer Jeremy Koh Kah Liam	32	5	59	–	4

Source: Design Studio's Annual Report 2010

problems compared to blue-chip companies. It is important for the management to admit mistakes candidly when they occur, outline the impact and key remedies to ensure complete mitigation and no repetition. For example, Warren Buffett candidly owned up to his mistakes in front of thousands of shareholders during an AGM in Omaha. He said this: "We will be candid in our reporting to you, emphasizing the pluses and minuses important in appraising a business. Our guideline is to tell you the business facts that we would want to know if our positions were reversed. We owe you no less."

Management should admit to their mistakes. (Note: Senior managers should do the honorable thing and fall on their swords.) Those who hide mistakes from investors and try to report positively every year should raise doubts among investors.

> We will be candid in our reporting to you, emphasizing the pluses and minuses important in appraising a business. Our guideline is to tell you the business facts that we would want to know if our positions were reversed. We owe you no less.
>
> —*Warren Buffett*

The mistakes can be candidly owned up to in the annual report's letter to shareholders, which is part of the reporting system. Such letters inform the shareholders of what happened in the previous financial years, mistakes made, and management's plans to bring the company forward. Reading this letter is a good way to get an insight in the character of those leading the company. To gauge the reporting system, investors must read this letter, which is written by the chairman, CEO, or managing director of the company, before investing in that company. Through this executive's own explanation of the business operations we will have a better feel for whether the chair is candid, consistent, and transparent in his or her message to shareholders. From our experience, some CEOs do not write the letter themselves; when we read such letters, there is no essence to them. We can't explain it how to spot it, but, by reading this letter, you should be able to feel the executive's style, which tends to be monotonous or a half-page letter without much explanation.

When the managers admits mistakes, they should address the problems as well and communicate contingency plans to overcome them so that they will not be repeated in future. You will also want to observe their body language when they share mistakes with investors during the AGM; the behavior and attitude displayed are likely to reflect how the board runs the company.

Criterion 3: Aligned with Shareholders' Interests

Conventionally, buying back shares using the company's excess cash is a good sign that management has their interests aligned with their shareholders. It is a good way to reward shareholders and maximize the stock value.

Buying back shares using the company's excess cash is a good sign that the management has its interests aligned with its shareholders.

There are two questions you have to ask yourself when management announces that they want to buy back shares using the company's funds: Is the company running out of growth opportunities to further expand its business? Or do they simply want to buy back shares to increase shareholders' value? The first question will require more thorough checking and investigation. Management may have misused the buyback shares strategy to create an illusion for investors that they are creating value by reducing the number of shares in the company. Consequently, it is likely to cause the share price to surge and create an opportunity for them to sell their stake at a profit. Watch out for this signal. It is definitely a good sign that the company is rewarding shareholders for their loyalty by holding the shares during an economic downturn. And this serves as an answer to the second question. For instance, it is a smart move to invest excess cash to purchase the company's shares if stocks worth $1 per share are trading at $0.50 per share. The same cannot be said if the stock is trading at $2 and management is still buying shares. Do not be surprised, as we have encountered managers who think that their shares, at price-to-earnings ratios (PEs) over 30, should trade even higher relative to the industry PE. In fact, it goes to show that management is not being rational in allocating capital for shareholders.

Generally, there are two types of share buying activities. The first is buying back shares using company's cash. Another is buying back shares through personal accounts. The latter is more encouraging than the former. Companies that buy back substantial amounts of shares from the market often give a good signal to investors that the stock is being sold at a bargain. Upon further analysis, if it is indeed undervalued, we are often enticed by the share buyback program. No one knows better what is going on in the company than management, who had bought huge amounts of shares through their personal accounts. So, it is worthwhile studying this carefully.

On the other hand, stock options are the additional shares issued to top-performing employees as a form of non-cash compensation. The reason why companies issue options is to make the employees (as part owners of the company) work even harder for the company by allowing them to use a small percentage of their salary to acquire new shares at discounted prices, and sometimes free. These will often increase the number of shares in the market and dilute the shareholders' percentage of shares in the company. Although it is minimal and regulated, some companies abuse this by issuing excessive new shares.

These options do not grant voting rights, but employees who hold option shares are entitled to dividends if they exercise the option. If the company gives out an excessive number of stock options to its employees, it raises red flags for investors. Using share options to add value to someone in the company is often not a good choice. We feel that true employees (who also think like an owner) should use their own cash to acquire the company's shares directly from the open market rather than at shareholders' expense. Watch out for CEOs or boards of directors who request additional new stock options to reward themselves when they already own a substantial stake in the company.

In 2010, for example, Design Studio did not issue any share options. This is definitely a good sign and is aligned to shareholders' interests because management does not intend to dilute existing shares.

Table 5.3 is extracted from Design Studio's 2009 annual report. They had raised additional new shares through convertible notes due to a lack of cash (a losing operation before 2006) to finance future growth. Once the company started to generate profits, they were able to maintain the number of outstanding shares for three consecutive years. Due to strong cash flow into business operations from 2006 onward, the company was able to fund its internal growth, thereby driving sales and net profits forward, without having to issue new shares again. In our opinion, they are likely to maintain the number of shares at least for

Table 5.3   Number of outstanding shares and cash & cash equivalent holding of Design Studio

Year	2005	2006	2007	2008	2009	2010
No. of Outstanding Shares (S$ million)	210.00	210.00	255.10	255.10	255.20	255.20
Cash & Cash Equivalent (S$ million)	−0.50	2.79	21.90	31.00	35.60	31.90

Source: Design Studio's Annual Report 2009

several years, unless the management opts for a stock split, as they have a strong cash base which allows them to readily expand and acquire new businesses.

Criterion 4: Track Record/Experience

This is a means by which to measure the credibility of management. The question to ask is, has the management met the objectives mentioned a few years ago? From the annual report, read the CEO's letter to shareholders to get some clues about the quality of the management. Whenever possible, compare this letter to that written five years back to check if the CEO, assuming he is still in place, has carried out all his plans. This is so you can see if the CEO's goals and objectives highlighted in the past have been executed or are aligned with the company's current direction. If he did implement the plan that was discussed earlier, it speaks favorably of the management's credibility and trustworthiness. Otherwise, he is expecting investors to forget what had been promised. And this is certainly not what we want of management. Action always speaks louder than words.

The shareholders' letter also serves as a good benchmark by which to assess management's ability and reputation. For instance, at Super Group Limited, the chairman had been talking about cost cutting and operations efficiency since 2005, as stated in the shareholders' letter. Year after year, its operations have become more efficient and expenses have decreased. This goes to show that the chairman is a man of his words. He meant what he said in the shareholders' letter and executed the plan to achieve it. And, in succeeding to do so, he has definitely benefitted the shareholders.

We also prefer a CEO who underpromises and overdelivers. If, through the latest letters and annual report, the CEO appears to be optimistic about the business yet sell stocks of the company, you will have to be extra careful. This is a classic pump-and-dump scenario (another share buyback scenario to misguide shareholders) in which management recommends their stocks to analysts, in the hopes of driving its price up, before selling it off for a quick profit. Conversely, you will also have to practice caution if the CEO sounds pessimistic and seems to be making excuses, blaming, or citing new challenges with no plans to overcome them. These are just some of the telltale signs you should look out for.

Although it is not our job as shareholders to hire management based on their experience and track record, it is equally important to spend some time reviewing the skills of the management team responsible for running the *Check whether the company has the same management in place or is constantly changing the management team.* company. Preferably, the senior management teams have relevant experience in the same or related industries. To determine this, browse the company's annual reports and read their backgrounds.

Check whether the company has the same management in place or is constantly changing the management team. After all, drastic changes in internal management can serve as a signal that the company is not able to retain high-quality talents. More often than not, it also reflects the internal working culture. When there is a change in management, look at the newly appointed directors to gauge their credibility and credentials, say, it could be the number of years of relevant experience in the same industry. For instance, when a shipping company appoints a new board of director with a lot of experience in the food and beverage industry, the real reason for the hire is more likely to be a personal choice (relationship) rather than a reflection of this person's ability to run the business. In which case, question the management about the decision.

Criterion 5: Visionary Managers

The success of any growth plan lies in the hands of management who envision themselves as achieving and creating value for shareholders. We know that investing is an art, because it requires investors to understand potential businesses are managed by capable people. The capability of these people is determined in the effective capital allocation of extra cash to create more value for shareholders and themselves. To fit the bill of growth companies, they have to invest money back into the business to ensure optimum and consistent growth rate of more than 15 percent over a few years. Thus, understanding management's vision and plan to expand the business in the future will determine whether the growth companies are worth holding in the long run. By that, we do not expect that managers must predict or give earnings guidance to analysts, but we are interested in their internal goals to grow the business. In fact, expect some fluctuation—no company has had earnings or revenue grow 15 percent linearly every year. Nevertheless, there are two strategies often used by a management to expand its business: organic growth and inorganic growth.

The ability to finance its growth needs internally suggests that the business is a good business because it has healthy cash flow.

Organic growth is the process of business expansion through the use of its own resources and assets. First, let us look at companies that fund internal growth using cash generated by the business. Using this approach, company does not need to issue new shares or borrow from banks. The ability to finance its growth needs internally suggests that the business is a good business because it has a healthy cash flow. Thus, the likelihood of this business being in the hands of a capable management is high. Over time, the market will reward these awesome managers because they continue to steer the company through tough times. This will increase the value of the company. For instance, OSIM announced it was opening 200 new stores in China. This is one of the growth strategies that management uses to venture into new markets. In this case, they find that there is much room to expand in a place like China. These are the facts covered by the management in their expansion plan.

In the AGM, bring up this question to the board: "Where do you see the company in the next five or ten years?" While we expect the answer to be optimistic, it should not be overly so. Also take note of management's body language when responding to the question. By doing so, you should have a good sense as to whether management is actually positive or negative about future business operations. Another question would be: "What are the initiatives being taken to grow the business further and increase shareholders' value?" This should reveal the steps being taken to improve the company's place in the market (e.g., upcoming products). It could also be an expansion plan through acquisitions. Again, future plans are usually covered in the annual report, which you can refer to.

When the company has reached its maximum growth, it is likely to use its excess cash to acquire another company to expand further. In other words, acquisition is done only when management has limited ideas as to how to grow the business internally or, simply, they see a huge potential in a company that they intend to acquire. This expansion process is known as *inorganic growth*. Acquisition is the strategy that is commonly used by companies to increase their revenue by buying a smaller company. In which case, management acquiring other companies to increase its value is definitely a good sign to shareholders. However, the problem lies in the price they pay to acquire the company and the difficulty of merging two different working cultures. Management must acquire the company at a reasonable price rather than one that could be detrimental to shareholders' value. Companies that keep acquiring many companies in a very short time serve as a warning sign to shareholders, as this usually happens when management is actually paying a high price for them. Hence, we should always keep a close lookout on how the company is using its cash to acquire companies.

This is also one of the concerns we have for Q&M Dental, which owned 37 clinics in Singapore in 2010, because they intend to open up to 60 and 50 clinics in Singapore and China, respectively, by 2015. Within this short period of time, we are worried that they might pay too much for some of the deals. In view of this, we have been monitoring them closely.

In addition, we prefer management to acquire companies that are related to their core business. By integration, this creates synergy and is a step closer to monopolizing the market. Here, consumer packaged goods firms should perhaps explore a company that manufactures plastics, something which is often used in packaging. Through vertical integration, dental companies, such as Q&M Dental, can create a strong synergy by acquiring a company that manufactures and performs research and development on dental products. This will serve the company well and enable it to gather higher gross profit margins, since it is able to produce products at a lower cost on its own. Depa, the world's largest interior fitting specialist, has acquired Design Studio, which is related to its core businesses of interior design, to increase its exposure in Asian markets, including China. It is a win-win opportunity for both companies.

Though we like the idea of vertical integration, which can bring down costs, research has shown that merger and acquisition (M&A) activities do not always produce the desire outcome. Nevertheless, some companies have in fact successfully integrated them. The palm oil industry in Asia, including Wilmar International, operates in a highly competitive environment with a razor-thin margin and has done exceptionally well through value chain integration.

Upon a successful acquisition, shareholders must be assured that the management team will be kept intact. In other words, the acquirer keeps the management team of the acquired organization locked in for at least a year. A good acquisition move made by Depa is that they kept the management unchanged after acquiring more than 90 percent of total shares. This is definitely a good sign for existing investors. If you see companies that intend to change management when the current management team's performance is good, pull yourself out of that investment. The reason for the change could be due to cultural clashes—a common problem in M&A. Remember, the goal of a successful value growth investor is to buy great businesses with trusted and unchanged management.

Philip Fisher's method is probably the best for judging the quality of a company's management. He suggests doing a scuttle-butting check by posing questions to the company's consumers, suppliers, and employees to get a good sense of the quality of management in terms of future growth. After carrying out this process, you can arrive at your own conclusions about the company's management. If any uncertainties arise about the management, you should avoid the company. In this case, scuttle-butting is a unique method of research that allows you to gain insight into the company and identify problems before the media or market is alerted to them.

A point to note is that an AGM would not normally be held on the company's premises. Thus, it does not provide investors an opportunity to do a ground check at the same time. By going directly to the company's headquarters, you are likely to see management in action. This is the place where they work, and is not often accessible to investors. However, some companies allow investors to pay a visit to the company. You can call the investor relations officer to check if you are allowed to visit the headquarters. By doing so, you can pick up warning signs if a company is badly run— such as freely spending shareholders' money on luxurious furniture. In such instances, investors should avoid these companies at all costs.

There are other sources of information by which one can find out about the management team. Analysts are paid to do research about specific companies and make recommendations to their clients. Analysts are likely to meet and talk to members of the management team when they are covering a specific company. They might not always provide honest opinions in their report, but it is one way to find out more about the company's businesses, management, and outlook. When analysts are silent about management's capabilities, chances are that the analysts know something about the company but would not or cannot reveal it, as they want to keep their jobs. Call your broker to see if the companies you are looking into have been covered in their analysis. However, do not be swayed by your broker. Remember, you are here to conduct your own research, not listen to one person's recommendations.

It is also a good idea to invest as a group, rather than alone. Sourcing and pooling information is much easier, as different people have access to different sources of information about management. A good starting point would be the Millionaire Investor Program (MIP), whereby you can network with more than 1,200 members who meet up quarterly for a networking night. In these meetings, management of different companies is invited to share company insights and attendees can ask questions directly face to face. We have friends from this network who have access to top executives of listed companies. Last, do a Google search on the CEO's full name. This is to check if there has been any bad publicity about the management team. Find out as much about the company as you can from different resources.

Once we have a good management team that is running a great business, we will be rewarded many times over if we stick with the investment in the long run. There are other factors that we should use to assess the real hands-on skill of a management. This will lead us to the next piece of the puzzle: numbers. This is management's scorecard and is mission critical in assessing how well the management team allocates and compounds shareholders' capital.

Summary

- Good management thinks and acts like an owner of the company. Good management reports candidly, be it on successes or mistakes, to shareholders and takes full responsibility for them.
- Good management receives compensation based on profit sharing.
- Good management should not adopt share options or issue additional shares when it is not needed.
- Good management is trustworthy and aligned to shareholders' interests.
- Good management holds a substantial amount of shares in the company.
- Good management is truly passionate about the business
- Good management constantly seeks ways to increase revenue and profit through yearly expansion.
- Good management makes its shareholders wealthier by buying back shares during crises when they are undervalued.

C H A P T E R

Numbers—The Third Piece of the Puzzle

Numbers Do Not Lie

In the last two chapters, we taught you how to look out for a good business that is poised for rapid growth and appears to be on track for rapid expansion if it is managed by an experienced and competent team. Now it is time to study the third piece of the puzzle, financial numbers or performance, to confirm if the business and its management have a good track record. These are real results, generated in the past.

When looking at growth companies, it is very important to monitor their revenue and earnings. They are key metrics used to track the success of a growth company. Companies that are able to consistently increase sales and profits should increase shareholders' value over time. It is important to know and understand these numbers, because they will help you understand how much profit the company is generating from its sales.

The fact is that the share price will, in the long run, reflect the growth of a company so long as it continues to deliver good results. This chapter will cover the fundamentals: numbers. Do note that we will not be going through the full accounts and its practices, that is, the rules and regulations (we leave these to regulators and accountants). However, as a value-growth investor, you will need to understand the basics of these accounting numbers and interpret these numbers from an investor's perspective. All the ratios that we will be sharing with you are not applicable to institutional organizations (e.g., bank or insurance firms) or cyclical entities. Now let us go through the financial statements of a business that sells widgets.

Numbers to Look at When Reading the Income Statement

Table 6.1 shows an example of an income statement.

Revenue

Revenue is commonly known as *sales* or *turnover* in accounting terms. It is reflected on the first line of the income statement. Money received from the sale of items will be recorded under revenue. Thus, the more products or services the company sells, the higher the revenue. From the previous income statement, the revenue is $11.3 million in 2009 (Table 6.2). It means the company sold $11.3 million worth of widgets in 2009. By looking at revenue alone, you cannot tell whether the company is profitable. However, a good growth company will show increases in revenue of more than 15 percent. For instance, in 2008 the revenue is $8.4 million. It grew by 34.5 percent, or $2.9 million, in 2009. This signaled a strong growth rate, because the company was able to sell more widgets than

Table 6.1 Example of income statement (financial year ended 31 December)

	(SGD '000)	
	2009	2008
Revenue	11,300	8,400
Cost of Goods Sold	(7,000)	(5,800)
Gross Profit	4,300	2,600
Expenses		
Marketing & Distribution	(634)	(410)
General & Admin	(950)	(770)
Depreciation	(150)	(140)
Exceptional Items	–	(400)
Operating Profit	2,566	880
Finance income	117	60
Tax	(383)	(210)
Net Profit	2,300	730
Earnings per Share (cents)	0.1	0.03

Table 6.2 Revenue in an income statement

	(SGD '000)	
	2009	2008
Revenue	**11,300**	**8,400**
Cost of Goods Sold	(7,000)	(5,800)
Gross Profit	4,300	2,600

before. A company with decreasing sales year to year is risky, because it is unable to sell more due to a drop in demand or increase in competition, where there are no moats protecting the business. Although revenue is a good indicator in determining whether a company is growing more than 15 percent a year, it cannot able to tell shareholders how profitable the company is. Thus, we need to find out how much the company is earning through selling widgets in 2009. A good rule of thumb is that the company should be able to grow its sales from 15 to 50 percent over three to five years.

A quick tip to determine annualized growth—any number that's doubled in five years' time is said to have grown at 15 percent or more. So, if revenue of $10 million grows to $20 million in five years, the annualized growth rate is 15 percent, and the company can thus be classified among growth companies.

Cost of Goods Sold

In order for this company to sell widgets, it is required to buy basic components, such as raw materials, component parts, wire, and so on. All the cost of making, shipping, and buying necessary materials to make its final products—widgets to sell to consumers in a particular year—will be recorded under Cost of Goods Sold.

From Table 6.3, we can see that, in 2009, the cost related to making the goods was $7 million, compared to its sales of $11.3 million. A company that sells products will normally have higher costs of goods because of the materials required to produce the final products. Conversely, a company that provides services to consumers will record lower costs of goods sold, because services tend to use lesser materials and require more manpower. For instance, VICOM, a vehicle inspection company in Singapore, provides servicing for cars; sales are recorded when it provides service. Thus, it is more labor intensive. By looking at this figure, we are able to know whether the company is a low-cost producer when compared to its competitors. The general rule is, the lower the cost, the more profit it will generate.

Gross Profit

To have a complete picture, investors need to calculate how much the company earns after deducting the costs of making the goods and selling it: gross profit. In this case, the formula to compute gross profit is:

$$\text{Gross Profit} = \text{Revenue} = \text{Cost of Goods Sold}$$

Table 6.3   Cost of goods sold in an income statement

	(SGD '000)	
	2009	**2008**
Revenue	11,300	8,400
Cost of Goods Sold	**(7,000)**	**(5,800)**
Gross Profit	4,300	2,600

For example, a normal widget sells for $50; the selling price is recorded under revenue. The cost of making each widget is $10. Therefore, the company earns $40 ($50–$10) of gross profit for each widget sold. From Table 6.4, the company made a gross profit of $4.3 million in 2009. Again, gross profit tells us very little about whether the company possesses any moats, just by looking at the figures. For this, we need something that we can measure against a company's gross profit. Thus, investors need to incorporate revenue to determine the percentage of its profitability: gross profit margin. This metric is one of the great formulas to determine whether a company is a low-cost producer among its competitors. The formula is:

$$\textbf{Gross Profit Margin}(\%) = \frac{\textbf{Gross Profit}}{\textbf{Sales}} \times 100\%$$

Based on information in Table 6.4, gross profit margin will be 38 percent. In other words, for every $100 in sales, the company earns $38 in gross profit. A good growth company

A sustainable good growth company will have a higher gross margin than its competitors.

should show a very high gross profit margin. This shows that they can charge a premium price to customers, because it can use the cheapest materials to produce and, at the same time, maintain product quality. A bad growth company that faces much competition tends to have very slim margins because, in order to survive, the company needs to offer the cheapest products by cutting prices. A competitive environment will have a tremendous impact on the gross profit margin since sales will drop, if cost of making the goods stays the same. However, there is no hard and fast rule for the gross

Table 6.4 Gross Profit in an income statement

	(SGD '000)	
	2009	2008
Revenue	11,300	8,400
Cost of Goods Sold	(7,000)	(5,800)
Gross Profit	4,300	2,600

profit margin of a growth company because it is dependent on the industry. In the food and beverage (F&B) industry, Japan Food has a gross profit margin of 77.5 percent, which is a higher gross profit margin than that of the manufacturing industry, where Armstrong Corp has a gross profit margin of 27.5 percent. Here, the bottom line is to compare gross profit margin with its competitors or against the industry's average. A sustainable good growth company will have a higher gross margin than its competitors.

It is very important that the company possesses a high margin because there are other expenses (e.g., advertising, wages) that have not been deducted from the recorded sales yet.

Expenses

Aside from production expenses (see Table 6.5), there are other expenses, such as marketing that a company might use to advertise its brand on television or in newspapers. Marketing expenses are, in most cases, economically necessary because the brand needs to create awareness and build a reputation with its target audience. The company also needs to hire employees to run its day-to-day operations, from highly paid executives to mailroom clerks. In this case, general and administrative expenses amounted to $950,000 in 2009. Additionally, machinery used to manufacture widgets depreciates due to wear and tear over time. This reflects its use over a determined useful life. In 2009, depreciation amounted

Table 6.5   Expenses in an income statement

	(SGD '000)	
	2009	2008
Expenses		
Marketing & Distribution	(634)	(410)
General & Admin	(950)	(770)
Depreciation	(150)	(140)
Exceptional Items	–	(400)
Operating Profit	2,566	880
Finance income	117	60
Tax	(383)	(210)
Net Profit	2,300	730

to $150,000, and it was deducted from the gross profit to show accuracy in earnings.

When the company borrows from a bank to run its business, it has to pay interest based on the amount borrowed within the financial year. It will not be shown in the income statement when the company has zero debt. A good growth company should not have high leverage or substantial loans to finance its daily operations. We will talk more about debts when we come to the topic on the balance sheet statement. In the meantime, when reading an income statement, investors should look out for any exceptional items. These items should be excluded from the calculations, be it a gain or loss, because it is a one-time event. However, if it is often repeated, it could be part of the operations, and investors should include them. In addition to such expenses, there are many other expenses that are not discussed in this book, as it would be too complicated and confusing to cover all of them.

The bottom line is that expenses have to be kept at their lowest. A good management team will attempt to keep expenses limited to a certain percentage of revenue. This can be accomplished through cost-cutting initiatives. In contrast, a company with bad management will likely allow expenses to spin out of control. This leads to higher expenses than initial gross profit. In other words, it suffers losses. Expenses are also commonly known as selling, general, and administrative expenses (SGA), excluding financial expense, taxes, and exceptional items. Some investors calculate the expense margin against revenue (expenses/revenue × 100%) or gross profit (expenses/gross profit × 100%) as a way to gauge consistency. We feel that, ultimately, doing so is needlessly time consuming because we can gauge the consistency using the profit margin as well. Here, when the profit margin is low, expenses are typically high and vice versa. Not to confuse you further, but let us discuss a little more about net profits.

Net Profit

The difference between the company's value this year and the previous year boils down to the amount of profit the business earns. Net profit can be found at the bottom line of the income statement and is commonly known as *net income* or *earnings*. It is derived by subtracting all the expenses (including costs of goods, finance expenses, tax, and other expenses) from revenue. The formula is:

Net Profit = Revenue − Cost of Goods Sold − Total Expenses

> The earnings will decide the fate of the stock.
>
> —*Peter Lynch*

In 2009, net profit generated amounted to $2.3 million. There was a huge increase from 2008 to 2009 due to a loss of exceptional items of $0.4 million. Since it was a one-time event, investors should include it back into the calculation to come up with more precise and accurate figures for 2008. After adding back the amount of $0.4 million, the net profit was $1.13 million in 2008. When the company reported a decrease in earnings—therein causing the share's price to plunge—Mr. Market suffered yet another mood swing, proving to be an opportune time for us to buy at a bargain price. Investors must be able to spot the occurrences of exceptional items and exclude them if they are one-time nonrecurring events. In this case, net profit increased by 104% in 2009.

Peter Lynch once said, "The earnings will decide the fate of the stock." Value-growth investors like to see an increase in reported earnings because it will increase the share price as well. Remember, share price always moves in tandem with earnings. A good growth company will increase its sales while still keeping its expenses at a minimum. The general rule for a good growth company is to grow its earnings at more than 15 percent over three to five years—an upward trend.

There are few ways a growth company can increase net profit:

1. Increase the price of services or products
2. Increase sales volume in the current market
3. Expand into overseas markets
4. Organic growth or via acquisitions plus innovation and introducing new products to generate new revenue streams
5. Control or reduce expenses to enhance margins

Calculating net profit will be more meaningful if we measure it against revenue. Here, net profit margin measures how much profit percentage a company makes for every $1 of sales. The formula is

Net Profit = Net Profit × 100% Revenue

From Table 6.6, the net profit margin derived is 20 percent ($2.3 million/$11.3 million × 100%). In other words, for every $1 of sales, the company made $0.20 in net profit.

Like gross profit margin, the preferable range for net margin also depends on the industry. Net profit margin varies from industry to industry and has to be compared against its competitors or industry's average. For instance, Japan Food had a net

Net profit margin varies from industry to industry and has to be compared against its competitors or industry's average.

profit margin of 10.5 percent in 2010, when the F&B industry's average stood at only 5 percent. This shows that it has a stronger franchise and can charge premium prices without losing its customers. It thus has great moats protecting it from competitors. In some cases, lower profit margin may mean two things: large economy of scale or price war. Being able to offer the same products to consumers at lower prices will be a good advantage over competitors. To do that, the company has to order stock in bulk or in huge volume. Companies like Noble Group, with a net profit margin of less than 2 percent, are also considered good growth companies because they possess scalability power—economy of scale. In other words, it might have a low margin but still be able to report high earnings due to its higher revenue. Noble reported S$42 billion and S$845 million in sales and net profit, respectively. The amount is too huge to ignore.

Conversely, a company is deemed a bad growth company when it gets involved in a price war. It must often compete with its competitors by lowering prices, which causes the margin to decrease as well. Creative Technology has shown continuous erosion in revenue and earnings because it has to reduce the price of its products to increase volume sales. In 2007, Creative Technology reported sales

Table 6.6 Net profit in an income statement

	(SGD '000)	
	2009	**2008**
Finance income	117	60
Tax	383	210
Net Profit	2,300	730

of S$1.4 billion with a net profit of S$41 million. In 2010, the company reported S$385 million in sales with a loss of S$53.7 million. In our opinion, technology companies face too much competition; it can be very hard to predict the future due to the nature of the industry. We would never invest in technology companies unless we have better insight into this industry. Ultimately, the higher the margin, the more competitive advantage it has.

Here, a good growth company should be able to show consistent profit margins. This shows that the management team has been taking control of its costs while rapidly expanding. Noble Group is a good example of this, as the management team was able to maintain a net profit margin from 2000 to 2010.

There are three signs that a growth company is having trouble maintaining its net profit margin:

1. Material or cost of goods sold increases
2. Company poorly manages its expenses
3. Competitors are lowering their prices, forcing the company to reduce its own as well

If a company shows signs that it is in a tight competitive war zone, it is likely that the company may not last long in the industry. Still, an understanding of the company's net profit margin is not conclusive as to whether a company is a good growth company. It would, at least, keep you away from companies that do not have a healthy net profit margin. Even if the company has net profits showing an upward trend of 15 percent per year, that alone is simply not enough reason to invest in a company. At times, growth companies might issue additional shares to raise capital during an aggressive expansion plan. Thus, we are required to determine a company's earnings per share due to an increase or decrease in outstanding shares.

Earnings per Share (EPS)

Here, EPS is used to determine the earnings for every share held by investors. It can be calculated as follows:

$$\text{EPS} = \frac{\text{Net Profit}}{\text{No. of Outstanding Shares}}$$

As shown in Table 6.7, in 2009, the widget business was earning 10 cents ($2.3 million ÷ 23 million) per share, assuming the number of outstanding shares is at 23 million. Given that the company experienced a one-time event in 2008, the actual net profit was $1.13 million, yielding an EPS (including exceptional items) of 4.91 cents ($1.13 million ÷ 23 million).

Companies that have consistent increases in profit do not necessarily bring value to the shareholders. We need to consider how actual earnings are delivered to shareholders based on the total number of shares issued (plus further dilution through stock options, outstanding warrants, and any convertible debt instruments). Growth companies in need of capital to finance growth tend to issue more shares during the rapid expansion phase. Thus, it will increase the total number of shares issued and potentially dilute EPS if there is not an offsetting increase in net profit growth. An indicator to track this situation is to obtain the EPS over the past five to 10 years.

Here, using EPS, there are three scenarios to be discussed. This is when net profit:

1. Increases, EPS increases
2. Increases, EPS decreases
3. Stays constant, EPS increases

First, when net profit increases, EPS should increase as well—they are directly proportionate to each other. This is the scenario that is preferred. Second, if net profit increases and EPS decreases, it can mean two things: The number of outstanding shares has increased either through an issuance of new shares (e.g., stock options, rights issue, or placement shares) or through a stock split.

Table 6.7 Earnings per share in an income statement

	(SGD '000)	
	2009	2008
Net Profit	2,300	730
EPS (cents)	0.1	0.03

Here, stock split is nondilutive, as investors still hold the same percentage in the company pre- and postsplit, whereas stock options, rights issues, convertible bonds, and placements are dilutive to minority shareholders if you do not purchase more shares to maintain your shareholding in the company. Last, we do not wish to invest if there is a decrease in profits (unless it is due to exceptional items) or when profits are stagnant for few years, as it will fail the margin test. A company with stagnant profits can still increase its EPS when the company buys back its own shares. A general rule is to keep a close watch on number of outstanding shares over a few years. Free shares issued to shareholders and stock splits are fine, but excessive share options or rights are not.

As investors, we should avoid any company that includes investment or paper gains in its income statement. This temporary gain should not be included in our calculation of earnings, as it is not part of the income from business operations. In relation to this, accounting rules require any nonrecurring, one-time income to be separated from income that comes from normal operations. Real estate companies or trusts, though not the focus of this book, are required to book valuation gains and losses from their properties. These are usually noncash items.

In 2009, Oceanus, an abalone producer and distributor, recorded sales of RMB362 million and total expenses (including taxes and finance charges) of about RMB320 million, when its net profit should have been RMB42 million (362–320). However, in the same year, it had reported a net profit of RMB339 million in the annual report. Why? This discrepancy was owing to a gain arising from changes in fair value in its biological assets (abalone), which totaled RMB651 million, and was included in the calculation of net profit in the income statement. Investors who do not study financial statements carefully would simply accept these reported earnings and make the assumption that the company is very profitable. But, as successful value-growth investors, we should exclude this gain because the changes in fair value were marked to the market but not sold yet. Thus, they should not be recorded in the calculation of net profit. Unless you know exactly what you are doing and are well versed in the value of these abalone, we would strongly encourage you to stay clear of them.

Numbers to Look at When Reading the Balance Sheet

On top of what has been discussed, there are also other numbers that you need to look out for when reading the balance sheet (see Table 6.8).

The purpose of the balance sheet is simple: to balance out the numbers on the debit and credit sides of the balance sheet. It is to show, at a specific point in time, the financial position of an organization. In the eyes of an investor, it denotes the current financial status of a company in that financial year. In a balance sheet, the total assets must always be equal to total liabilities plus

Table 6.8   Example of balance sheet

Assets	(SGD '000) 2009	2008	Liabilities	(SGD '000) 2009	2008
Noncurrent Assets			Noncurrent Liabilities		
Property, Plant, & Equipment	4,900	3,130	Long-Term Bank Loan	–	–
Long-Term Investment	100	70	Other Liabilities	1,350	900
	5,000	3,200		1,350	900
			Current Liabilities		
			Trade & Other Payables	3,500	1,900
Current Assets			Accrued Expenses	650	450
Cash & Cash Equivalent	3,900	2,000		4,150	2,350
Inventory	500	250			
Trade & Other Receivables	4,000	3,100	Shareholders' Equity		
Prepaid Expenses	1,600	1,400	Share Capital	3,000	3,000
	10,000	6,750	Retain Earnings	6,000	3,200
			Minority Interest	500	500
Total Assets	15,000	9,950		9,500	6,700

shareholders' equity. There are fundamentally three parts: assets, liabilities and shareholders' equity. The equation is as follow:

$$\text{Assets} = \text{Liabilities} + \text{Shareholders' Equity}$$

Here, assets can be broken into two parts—noncurrent and current assets.

$$\text{Total Assets} = \text{Noncurrent Assets} + \text{Current Assets}$$

Liabilities can also be further broken into two parts—noncurrent and current liabilities.

$$\text{Total Liabilities} = \text{Noncurrent Liabilities} + \text{Current Liabilities}$$

Here, it is not the investor's job to know where each item should be recorded, but to know what numbers to look out for when reading the balance sheet. Just as in an income statement, the numbers in the balance sheet do not make sense without projecting some ratio to compare one with the other. Before computing the ratio, it is then important to spend some time understanding what these numbers are and why they are there.

Noncurrent Assets

Using the example discussed earlier, a widget business requires machinery to process raw materials into final products. In addition, it also requires space to sell widgets to consumers. Thus, it needs a building in order to start its business operation and a place for its central office. These are fixed assets that are likely to last more than a year and therefore are recorded under noncurrent assets.

Companies selling services to consumers are less asset intensive than companies that require factories to manufacture products. The amount is often recorded at *cost price*—the initial price paid for securing the use of the asset. For example, if a company purchased a building and factory for $4.9 million, then the historic cost of these assets is $4.9 million (Table 6.9). As time goes by, the equipment contributes to the firm in terms of generating economic benefits, as its cost depreciates over its useful life (e.g., 10 years). This depreciation charge will be recorded in the income statement

Table 6.9   Noncurrent assets in a balance sheet

	(SGD '000)	
	2009	2008
Noncurrent Assets		
Property, Plant, & Equipment	4,900	3,130
Long-Term Investment	100	70
	5,000	3,200

to determine the true profit from its operations. Do note, however, that this is a noncash item and its useful life can be changed at the management's discretion, which would increase or decrease reported net profit. A good business will not need to go through major changes in the future. In other words, the company does not have to constantly upgrade or redesign its machinery in order to stay ahead. In doing so, it helps save shareholders' money and, at the same time, creates more profits that can be returned to its shareholders.

Here, a growth company with a long-term investment tells us something about its management. This proves that management is continuously increasing shareholders' value by looking into new investments to generate more profits. It could be in the form of an acquisition in another company or bonds. However, some groups buy new companies or perform corporate takeovers just to increase their power and influence. This often demands high prices that destroy shareholders' value. As mentioned previously, a good management team will likely acquire a business that is related to its core business at a reasonable price. Since Q&M Dental is involved in providing dental services to consumers, it is more logical for them to acquire a firm that produces dental equipment. This will create synergies that potentially lower the cost of equipment. But if Q&M Dental decides instead to acquire an F&B business, this would be what Peter Lynch calls *diworsification,* In this case, diworsification might cause earnings to drop, especially if the newly acquired business fails to perform. This will hurt shareholders' interests when they try to focus on something they are not well versed in. On the balance sheet, long-term investments can be found under noncurrent assets. If this balance is big, you may want to dig into the details to ensure that you are comfortable with the kind of risks that the management is taking with its shareholders' money.

Other items recorded under noncurrent assets include intangible assets, goodwill, deferred tax assets, and so on. Growth companies should have a negligible amount recorded here. And, if amounts are recorded, it is best to evaluate them carefully. For instance, a high level of goodwill (derived from the difference between the purchase price and net asset value) indicates that the company is paying a premium over its book value when making an acquisition. Typically, the smaller the figure, the better the company is.

Current Assets

While noncurrent assets cannot be converted into cash within a period of one year, current assets can be converted into cash within a year.

In Table 6.10, the cash and cash equivalent amounts to $3.9 million. This means the company is highly liquid and is able to support its ongoing day-to-day operations and tide itself over through short-term problems. Conversely, companies short of cash will have a tough time when a crisis hits and often end up borrowing money from the bank or issuing additional new shares. Value-growth investors love to see cash in the balance sheet. The higher the amount, the better it is. When companies reach their limit to expand further, they will likely pay it out as dividends. A good management team will also buy back shares when they feel the company is undervalued, to create more value to shareholders. Generally, growth companies tend to use the money to finance operations in the form of expansion, in order to generate more returns, instead of paying

Table 6.10   Current assets in a balance sheet

| | (SGD '000) | |
	2009	2008
Current Assets		
Cash & Cash Equivalent	3,900	2,000
Inventory	500	250
Trade & Other Receivables	4,000	3,100
Prepaid Expenses	1,600	1,400
	10,000	6,750

a dividend. Here, a general rule is to see a growth in cash for the past five years.

Also a current asset, inventory refers to the raw materials needed to produce widgets, as

well as the finished products that are ready for sale. In this case, the company has $500,000 worth of inventory to produce the needed amount or sell the ready-made widgets within a period of one year. Inventory is only applicable to companies that sell goods; it is less applicable to companies that provide a service. For instance, it does not make sense to categorize a postman under inventory just because he provides a service to customers by delivering mail.

When inventories start to grow but revenue decreases, this causes problems. It could mean that the company is having a hard time selling off its stocks or that the stocks are no longer in demand, therein suggesting a loss of competitive advantage. A very good example is the information technology industry, in which technology quickly becomes obsolete. When a new and enhanced gadget becomes available, older gadgets become hard to sell. At this stage, companies can sell the inventories at a discounted price, often below their cost price. Here, sales should be directly proportional to inventory. Otherwise, check for some sort of explanation in the annual report.

Trade and other receivables are also current assets. They can also be referred to as *debtors* in the balance sheet. In this case, money is owed to the company after the company sells its goods; it takes some time to receive the money. Here, a company can still increase its sales when it allows credit terms (e.g., three months) to be made available to its debtors. It is also a common way to manipulate sales.

Goods or services are still provided, even though customers pay back later. Not all receivables can be collected, because some might not be able or are unwilling to pay. When it is not collected, it becomes bad debt. And this has to be written off as a loss in operation. If receivables are rising faster than sales, it means that companies are reporting more sales by offering longer credit terms to their debtors. This is a common practice of sales manipulation by reporting sales through longer credit terms. As investors, we can compare trade receivables and sales to spot this trend of sales manipulation.

There are other current assets, such as prepaid expenses. These are the expenses not incurred but paid in advance and recorded on the balance sheet.

Noncurrent Liabilities

Noncurrent liabilities are the flip side of noncurrent assets. They refer to long-term bank loans that may be paid after a period of longer than a year, where all loans are subject to interest rates. Generally, too much long-term debt is risky, as the debt and interest charged for the debt must be repaid no matter how the business fares. When such loans are incurred, they are typically recorded as finances or interest expenses on the income statement. Although there are other noncurrent liabilities, long-term bank loans are the most important ones to look at. Table 6.11 shows noncurrent liabilities in a balance sheet.

Companies that have high levels of borrowing are likely to face more problems and have trouble repaying them when a crisis hits.

It is best to avoid growth companies using high long-term bank loans to finance their rapid expansion because eventually, the debt has to be paid off. This will likely create cash-flow issues when not enough cash is available. On the other hand, a good growth company should have little or no debt. In this case, this company does not require high debt to finance its growth. There are, of course, other liabilities, such as deferred tax liability. (Note: The general rule of thumb is to see a decline in debts in the past five years. This indicates that the management team is making an effort to pay off its long-term debt.)

Table 6.11   Noncurrent liabilities in a balance sheet

	(SGD '000)	
	2009	2008
Noncurrent Liabilities		
Long-Term Bank Loan	–	–
Other Liabilities	1,350	900
	1,350	900

Current Liabilities

Current liabilities simply refer to payments, borrowing, and debts owed to creditors that have to be paid within a year. As we discussed earlier, such liabilities are incurred when the widget owner orders its materials from the supplier on credit and it is recorded as payables.

Trade and other payables are a current liability when they are simply the opposite of trade receivables. Put simply, this refers to money owed to the supplier. Meanwhile, accrued expenses are debts that are incurred by a company but for which payment has not yet been made. These are normally periodic expenses, such as wages and rents that are not yet due. For instance, the company hires additional staff to look after its day-to-day operations. In which case, wages are incurred that need to be paid at the end of the month. But, before wages are actually paid, they are first recorded as an accrued expense.

Apart from trade and other payables and accrued expenses, short-term debt is another short-term liability. Here, short-term debt is incurred when a company borrows long-term debt from the bank. Initially, this will be recorded under non-current liabilities. But, when it is about to come due, the amount will become a current liability as a short-term debt. If the company is unable to pay off the debt within that year, it could face the fate of shutting down or be forced to sell its assets at fire-sale prices.

Contrary to popular belief, growth companies are not necessarily those that do not incur any debts. In fact, growth companies are likely to use some debts to finance day-to-day operations and expansion when it decides not to issue additional shares. For example, Design Studio had total borrowing (short- and long-term debt) of $7 million in 2006. However, the debt was fully repaid in 2010. In this case, it is clear that the management team was committed to pay off its debts to avoid possible trouble. As noted earlier, the general rule is to see a declining trend in borrowing over a period of five years. Table 6.12 shows current liabilities in a balance sheet.

Table 6.12 Current liabilities in a balance sheet

	(SGD '000)	
	2009	2008
Current Liabilities		
Trade & Other Payables	3,500	1,900
Accrued Expenses	650	450
	4,150	2,350

Shareholders' Equity

Shareholders' equity is commonly known as *book value* or *net assets*. It is the difference between total assets and total liabilities, or the equivalent of the total net worth of a company. This is the amount of money being placed into the company to keep the business running, with additional profits generated and retained. Table 6.13 shows shareholders' equity in a balance sheet.

Before starting the widget business, the owner invested initial capital of $1 million to set up the operation. This initial capital amount will be recorded as share capital under shareholders' equity. Publicly listed companies raise capital in exchange for issuing additional shares to retail investors. For instance, if a widget business intends to go for an initial public offering (IPO) in order to raise an additional $2 million from outside shareholders, it will issue 10 million shares at $0.20 each share. This makes a total of $3 million of paid-up capital and is recorded in the share capital. When companies make a profit after deducting all the expenses, dividends, and buying back shares, this amount will be added into retained earnings as part of income and value creation to shareholders. Since the effective date of operation, the widget business has generated total retained earnings of $6 million to shareholders. Likewise, when a company loses money, it will subtract the amount from retained earnings. Value-growth investors like to look at retained earnings to see if the amount has been consistently increasing over the years, because that implies that the net worth of the company is also increasing.

Value-growth investors like to look at retained earnings to see if the amount has been consistently increasing over the years.

Table 6.13   Shareholders' equity in a balance sheet

	(SGD '000)	
	2009	2009
Shareholders' Equity		
Share Capital	3,000	3,000
Retain Earnings	6,000	3,200
Minority Interest	500	500
	9,500	6,700

We prefer a growth company to retain as much earnings as possible for it to expand its business. Especially in the case of smaller growth companies, when the management—with chief executive ownership of more than 50 percent of shares—continually declares high dividends, instead of redirecting the money to finance its expansion, it is really as good as the owner taking the money and putting it into his own pocket. If this happens, it implies that management is not interested in creating value for its shareholders and has no intention to grow. If they are interested in the shareholders' value, they should retain the earnings and expand the business to drive earnings further.

Minority interest is a noncontrolling interest. It refers to the portion of a subsidiary corporation's stock that is not owned by the parent corporation. For instance, if Widget Business Owner A contributes $500,000 to partner Owner B, whose contribution is $100,000, to open up a new branch, Owner B is said to be the minority interest because he does not own direct shares in the company. In this case, Owner B's contribution tends to be negligible among the majority of the growth companies. When calculating total shareholders, investors need to exclude them (if the amount is too large), because minority interest immediately receives profits when earnings are recorded. This is normally reflected in the last line of the income statement.

Current Ratio

The current ratio is used to test a company's financial strength to determine its ability to meet short-term debt obligations. It calculates how many dollars in total assets are likely to be converted to cash within one year, in order for a company to pay off its debts in the same period.

$$\text{Current Ratio} = \frac{\text{Current Assets}}{\text{Current Liabilities}}$$

For example, in 2009, current assets and current liabilities of the widget business was at $10 million and $4.15 million, respectively. Its current ratio worked out to be 2.4 ($10 million/$4.15 million), meaning it had 2.4 times more current assets than current liabilities. These figures imply that the company was liquid enough to meet its short-term debt. If the current ratio was 1, then it implies that the company had more current assets than current liabilities.

Having a high current ratio is especially important for growth companies, as they are constantly expanding. In doing so, they are using cash flow to generate and bring in more risks in the short term. These companies have to be liquid enough to withstand a crisis. In contrast, mature companies do not have to constantly reinvest their money to finance growth as they have a strong cash flow.

Return on Equity

One of the most important profitability ratios in determining a good growth company is return on equity (ROE). By calculating a company's ROE, investors will be able to determine how much money they are getting back for every dollar of invested capital. ROE will be able to measure the ability of the management team in utilizing shareholders' investments in the company. It is a measure of value creation by the management for the shareholders. If they can invest capital in the business and generate a rate of return that exceeds the cost of that capital, value is created for the shareholders.

$$\text{Return on Equity} = \frac{\text{Net Profit}}{\text{Shareholders' Equity}} \times 100\%$$

From the income statement, net profit amounted to $2.3 million and, on the balance sheet, shareholders' equity amounted to $9.5 million. As such, ROE worked out to be around 24 percent ($2.3 million/$9.5 million × 100 percent). This means that for every dollar of shareholders' money, they were getting back $0.24.

In relation to this point, a growth company with high ROE is more likely to be one that is able to generate cash internally, meaning that the company is self-sufficient. A general rule of thumb is to find companies that have an ROE of a minimum of 15 percent. Having said that, there are also good growth companies that may report a lower–than–15 percent ROE but maintain a consistent growth from year to year. While they may seem to have a low ROE at the start, the management is able to improve the ROE from year to year, as shown in Table 6.14.

Table 6.14   Company with increasing ROE

Year	2005	2006	2007	2008	2009
Return on Equity (%)	6	9	11	13	15

If a company's ROE does improve from year to year, it is likely to be a potential growth company that would produce a multi-bagger return. As such, investors cannot look at rising per-share earnings each year as a sign of success alone. ROE takes into account retained earnings from previous years and tells investors how effectively their capital is being reinvested. ROE is a more accurate indicator when determining the management team's capability in handling shareholders' money. Should your personal goal be to grow your own investment by at least 15 percent per year, then we recommend that you invest only in companies with ROEs of at least 15 percent.

We also have to be wary when a company's ROE is exceptionally high (e.g., 80 percent or more). In this case, there are few possible reasons why the ROE is high:

1. One-time gain (exceptional items) makes net profit surge
2. Lower shareholders' equity when management buys back shares
3. Highly financed by debts

There are other possible reasons, such as substantial profit generated from the subsidiaries, and so on. We shall look at the first reason, a nonrecurring, one-time event of earnings, possibly obtained from a sale of a property or a plant. As such, the high ROE will not be sustainable in the following year. Investors should exclude this during the calculation of net profit, when necessary, to reveal the true ROE. Here, a consistent or increasing ROE is a key metric to our decision when determining whether a company is a growth company. A high ROE could also mean there is share buyback activity in the company. Now, this is a reason to investigate further. If net profit increases steadily with an additional share buyback during a downturn, it is a good sign to investors because it increases shareholders' value. The amount is recorded as treasury shares on the balance sheet.

On the other hand, if the main motive of the share buyback is to keep the ROE high, but the net profit has stagnated or decreased, it could be a sign that the company is simply trying to keep the ROE high so as to attract more investors who think that the company is giving a good return on investment. However, growth companies are unlikely to buy back shares unless the management does not know what to do with the cash in hand. In which case, it is good to buy during downturns and increase shareholders' value. But, if the management insists on buying back shares when they are overvalued, then chances are high that the management is running out of ideas as to how to grow the business.

As in the case for net profit margin, good growth companies should produce higher ROEs than the industry's average or that of competitors. But, sad to say, the computation of ROE has some limitations: It cannot be used as a metric for comparison within the same industry since it ignores the effect of debts. This makes our comparison, be it with competitors or industry's average, misleading. In fact, most companies would fit the bill of having more than 15 percent ROE, as it is mainly financed by debts. Thus, it is quite important we augment this analysis by considering metrics that factor in debts.

And it is best to use it along with the next ratio—debt to equity.

Debt-to-Equity Ratio

Debt to equity is also known as *gearing*. Debts, in this case, refer to short- and long-term bank loans.

$$\textbf{Debt-to-Equity Ratio} = \frac{\textbf{Total Debt}}{\textbf{Shareholders' Equity}}$$

The lower the ratio is, the less risk of failure or bankruptcy. This will significantly reduce our risks and preserve our capital in the long run. Growth companies with low debt indicate that the company's operations are financed internally, through earnings from operations. In short, companies do not need to take out bank loans to keep the operation running. The debt to equity ratio is zero because the widget business does not borrow any money from banks to finance its operations. As investors, the preferred ratio for debt-to-equity ratio is capped at 0.5 (see Table 6.15).

Why is total debt used instead of total liabilities? As mentioned earlier, debts refer to bank loans. For total liabilities, its computation includes amounts owing to suppliers or creditors. In legal terms, the money that is owed to the bank has to be paid first in times of

Table 6.15 Three different companies with the same ROE of 25 percent

	Company A	Company B	Company C
Sales ($ million)	20.0	20.0	20.0
Net Profit ($ million)	3.0	2.0	1.0
Borrowing ($ million)	0.0	4.0	8.0
Shareholders' Equity ($ million)	12.0	8.0	4.0
Return on Equity (%)	25.0	25.0	25.0
Debt to Equity	0.0	0.5	2.0

crisis, as a default will place the company in a dire state, and banks are quick to take action against any default. Regarding payables to creditors, most creditors do not take action immediately, for fear of losing the client if they do. Thus, high leverage in a company can lead to financial problems. A low debt-to-equity ratio in a company is an important indication of a strong balance sheet. A good example of a highly leveraged company is TT International, as it was in the center of a raging legal battle with creditors in 2010. This problem started during the financial crisis, when it found itself under a mountain of debts and had trouble repaying creditors.

Generally speaking, companies with higher debts, as measured using a debt-to-equity ratio, will have high ROEs as well. To have a better understanding of ROE and a gearing relationship, take a look at Table 6.15, and decide which company you would rather invest your money in.

All three companies produce the same ROE of 25 percent. Between the three companies, investors will definitely choose Company A because its management is able to maximize shareholders' money without borrowing from the bank and with zero gearing. Though Company C is also able to produce an ROE of 25 percent, it is not a good growth company because it has a high debt-to-equity ratio of 2, and would place our money at risk if there were a catastrophic event. If investors use ROE alone to identify a good company or to make a comparison with its competitors, it will prove to be dangerous and inaccurate. In conclusion, ROE is more effective when it is used alongside a debt-to-equity ratio. In doing so, the true potential growth company will be revealed!

ROE is more effective when it is used alongside a debt-to-equity ratio.

Numbers to Look at When Reading the Cash-Flow Statement

While income statements can be cloaked in mystery (i.e., revenue can be recorded even though the cash has not been received), due to an accrual system where transactions can be recorded as credit terms, the cash-flow statement is more straightforward; it is what it is: real cash inflow and outflow. With a cash-flow statement, we can easily see how much cash is generated by the company's operating activities, as well as how it is spent. While some managers maximize cash flow and distribute it efficiently among new projects, share repurchases, and dividend payments, other managers might make terrible acquisitions or incur unnecessary expenses. As shown in Table 6.16, a cash-flow statement is nicely broken down into three segments: cash flow from operations, cash flow from investing, and cash flow from financing activities.

Table 6.16   Example of cash-flow statement

	(SGD '000)	
	2009	2008
Cash flows from Operating Activities		
Net Profit	2,300	730
Depreciation	150	140
Exceptional Items	–	400
Interest Income	(117)	(60)
Operating Profit before Working Capital	2,333	1210
Inventories	(250)	120
Trade & Other Receivables	(993)	(200)
Trade & Other Payables	1,800	250
Net cash flows from operating activities	2890	1380
Cash flows from Investing Activities		
Purchase of Property, Plant, & Equipment	(560)	(310)
Other Investment	(30)	–
Net Cash Used in Investing Activities	(590)	(310)
Cash Flows from Financing Activities		
Bank Loan	–	(50)
Dividend Paid	(400)	(250)
Net Cash Used in Financing Activities	(400)	(300)
Begin Cash & Cash Equivalent	2,000	1,230
End Cash & Cash Equivalent	3,900	2,000

Cash Flow from Operations

The purpose of assessing cash flow from operating activities is to determine a company's true earnings through business operations. To reflect the actual cash flow of the business, the net profit amount of $2.3 million is being brought forward from the income statement to the top line of the cash-flow statement, as shown in Table 6.17, where some adjustments are made. In contrast with the income statement, the function of a cash-flow statement is to track the actual movement of cash inflow and outflow of a business operation. Since depreciation and exceptional items do not involve any movement of cash, these amounts would be added back to the net profit amount (where these figures were initially deducted in the income statement). And, since an interest income of $0.117 million from the bank is not part of operational profits, it is taken out in order to determine the true operating profits before we finally derive a working capital of $2.33 million.

Since depreciation and exceptional items do not involve any movement of cash, these amounts would be added back into the net profit amount (where these figures were initially deducted from income statement).

Here, note how it works backward from net profit. In the same year, the company spent $0.25 million to acquire more inventory for sales; this amount has been deducted. Since some of the

Table 6.17 Cash-flow from operations in cash-flow statement

	(SGD '000) 2009	2008
Cash Flow from Operating Activities		
Net Profit	2,300	730
Depreciation	150	140
Exceptional Items	–	400
Interest Income	(117)	(60)
Operating Profit before Working Capital	2,333	1210
Inventories	(250)	120
Trade & Other Receivables	(993)	(200)
Trade & Other Payables	1,800	250
Net Cash Flow from Operating Activities	2890	1380

revenue has been recorded even though the cash has not been received, it must also be taken out from trade and other receivables. Trade and other payables or creditors have also increased by $1.8 million in 2009, because money owed to the suppliers has not been paid to them. After all the necessary addition and subtraction, we end up with $2.89 million. In this case, this computation is commonly known as *operating cash flow* (OCF). In annual reports, it is sometimes shown as net cash flow from operating activities. They refer to the same thing, even though they are given different accounting terms. Here, the rule is to have an OCF amount higher than earnings. This tells us that the company is actually earning more than is being reported.

Cash Flow from Investment

Purchases of property, plants, and equipment are known as *capital expenditure*, or CAPEX. In Table 6.18, this expenditure amounted to $0.56 million in 2009. This is the money spent to fix, upgrade, or acquire physical assets, such as properties, plants, and equipment, in order to grow and keep the business going in the long run. It is a negative figure, as money had been taken out of the business. In this case, the company made a small investment, which amounted to $30,000, in the hope that it would lead to future growth in earnings. This would, at the same time, increase the investment in the balance sheet statement by the same amount. As a result, the total cash used in investing activities was $0.59 million. Here, investors have to pay close attention to CAPEX.

Essentially, CAPEX is part of maintenance and development costs. Maintenance CAPEX refers to the money spent in order to maintain the economic moats of a business. In retail business,

Table 6.18 Cash flow from investment in cash-flow statement

	(SGD '000)	
	2009	**2008**
Cash Flow from Investing Activities		
Purchase of Property, Plant, & Equipment	(560)	(310)
Other Investment	(30)	–
Net cash used in investing activities	(590)	(310)

many companies are willing to spend on renovation cost just to stay afloat in a highly competitive industry. For a growth company, a high CAPEX is normal, as the company needs huge capital (development costs) to expand its business. It has to justify this with an increase in revenue and net profit. A CAPEX value that is consistently high, but does not lead to high growth, is likely to be maintenance cost. A way to determine whether a company is overspending is by comparing its CAPEX with net profit. This shows the level of expense that needs to be put back for every dollar earned.

$$\text{CAPEX Ratio} = \frac{\text{Capital Expenditure}}{\text{Net Profit}} \times 100\%$$

From the example of widget business, the CAPEX ratio is 19.3 percent ($0.56 million/$2.89 million × 100%). In other words, for every $1 dollar earned, the company has to put back $0.20 to keep the business running and growing. The general rule is to have this ratio at less than 80 percent. If the percentage is over 100 percent, it could mean that the company is spending too much on CAPEX and, as a result, needs to borrow money or issue additional new shares. This is common in growth companies, where they need to spend more than the profit they generate. If companies do not need to continually upgrade their property and machinery, but are still able to increase earnings and sales, they will create more profit for shareholders.

For instance, in 2009, Design Studio was still able to increase its sales and earnings by more than 40 percent without overspending whatever profits it made in 2008. In this case, its CAPEX ratio was only at 11.5 percent! During the same year, Boustead, with a CAPEX ratio of 17.9 percent, was able to increase its sales and earnings by more than 15 percent. On the other hand, there are growth companies that need to spend high CAPEX in order to drive their revenue and earnings upward. For instance, BreadTalk had a CAPEX ratio of more than 300 percent in 2008! At first glance, this may scare investors off. But, upon further investigation, we are interested in BreadTalk because of one important number: free cash flow (FCF).

To better determine OCF, investors should look at figures such as FCF. FCF is the money left after paying the cost of doing business, upkeep and maintenance needed to stay in business, or capital expenditure. The formula is

Free Cash Flow = Operation Cash Flow − Capital Expenditure

A good growth company should have a positive FCF.

To understand FCF better, let us give you an example. If you earn $3,000 every month and, in order to survive, you need to spend $2,000 on basic expenses (i.e., food, transport, utilities, car), the $1,000 left over is your positive cash flow, or FCF. This money can be used to invest in the stock market to earn even more income in the future or simply used for a vacation. However, if your expenses are greater than your income (i.e., $4,000), you will have problems covering your basic expenses, because you will need an additional $1,000 to offset them. To cover these expenses, you could borrow money from the bank or from relatives. Similarly, companies may face the same scenario when they incur expenses, such as maintenance costs and development costs. If the company's FCF is negative, it would have to look for ways to raise the money by either borrowing or offering additional new shares. If the FCF is positive, the company is self-reliant and is able to launch new ventures without borrowing money, or create more value to shareholders through share buyback or dividends. A good growth company should have a positive FCF.

Earlier, we mentioned that BreadTalk has a CAPEX ratio of more than 300 percent. Surprisingly, it is still generating a positive FCF of S$8.9 million. In other words, BreadTalk is reporting a lower net profit of S$11.2 million compared to its OCF of S$45.4 million. In fact, it is generating more cash than that which appears on the face of its income statement! Thus, it does not have to issue additional shares to raise capital. This spending is also justified by its increase in revenue of S$302 million in 2010. That is more than 22 percent increase from the previous year, when revenue stood at $246 million. In view of this, you must be able to relate CAPEX ratio to FCF to get a clearer picture of a company. If the CAPEX is too high and FCF is negative, you should do your best to avoid the company as it is consuming more cash than it is taking in. Chances of the company issuing new shares or borrowing more money are high if this persists.

Cash Flow from Finance

Finally, we need to monitor the movement of cash in financing activities, as this figure contributes to our passive income, dividends. As mentioned previously, a good growth company—one that has the ability to sustain itself—is unlikely to borrow money to finance its operations. As a shareholder, we do not want profits to be eroded by debt payments. Bank loans should be at a minimum or even zero.

In the example of the widget business, the company paid out a dividend of $350,000 in cash to existing shareholders. This number alone will not make sense if we do not relate it to net profits. A dividend ratio is a way to measure how much dividend is given out for every dollar of profit.

Dividend Payout Ratio = Dividend Paid to Shareholders × 100%

The dividend payout ratio is 15.2 percent ($0.35 million/2.3 million × 100%). A growth company will typically pay lesser dividends than mature companies, as growth companies need more money to expand compared to slow-growing companies. Growth companies tend to retain their cash rather than pay it out as dividends.

With this understanding, while most investors like to receive thick dividends, it is wiser for the capable management team to place the money back into the business and compound it further. As investors, we need to look for a consistent dividend payout ratio to maintain the dividend sustainability, much like that in Table 6.20, so that our dividend will grow as well.

Table 6.19   Cash flow from finance in cash-flow statement

	(SGD '000)	
	2009	2008
Cash Flow from Financing Activities		
Bank Loan	–	(50)
Dividend Paid to Shareholders	(350)	(230)
Dividend Paid to Minority Interest	(50)	(20)
Net Cash Used in Financing Activities	(400)	(300)
Begin Cash and Cash Equivalent	2,000	1,230
End Cash and Cash equivalent	3,900	2,000

In relation to this, let us look at the example of Boustead and Design Studio in Table 6.21.

We need to look out for a consistent dividend payout ratio to maintain the dividend sustainability.

As investors, we are not expecting a dividend ratio of more than 50 percent for growth companies. But as long as they can maintain the dividend ratio, we should be assured that our dividend will grow as well. As it is, a growth company that can maintain its dividend payout ratio at less than 50 percent for the past five years is said to have healthy dividends paid to shareholders, because it can channel the remaining profit back into the business to increase shareholders' value with a high ROE through higher revenue and profit. If management pays too high a dividend (e.g., 80 percent), it may be a sign that it is running out of growth ideas. Thus, it turns to rewarding the shareholders with cash in the form of dividends.

We need to look out for healthy dividend payouts (consistent for the past five years) instead of high dividend yields that use up more than 100 percent of what the company earns to be paid out as dividends. It can be misleading if investors only focus on high dividend yield stocks.

Table 6.20   Dividend ratio from years 2005 to 2009

	2005	2006	2007	2008	2009
Revenue ($ million)	10.0	12.0	14.0	16.5	18.0
Net Profit ($ million)	1.5	1.8	2.2	2.6	3.1
Dividend ($ million)	0.5	0.65	0.8	0.9	1.0
Dividend Ratio (%)	33.0	36.0	36.0	34.0	32.0

Table 6.21   Dividend ratios for Boustead and Design Studio from years 2005 to 2009

Boustead	2005	2006	2007	2008	2009
Dividend Ratio	24%	17%	33%	42%	46%
Design Studio	**2005**	**2006**	**2007**	**2008**	**2009**
Dividend Ratio	0	0	10.3%	19.6%	26.9%

Ultimately, the cash-flow statement is created because investors need to know how much cash and cash equivalent is left at the end (after addition of cash inflow and subtraction of cash outflow). This figure can be found on the last line of the cash-flow statement. As a value-growth investor, we like to see cash and cash equivalent increase year after year. However, when it does decrease, we should find out what happened. We should not be overly alarmed, as this drop might be due to some form of acquisition in a particular year or just more dividends being paid out.

Last, numbers in a financial report are never to be used as is. Rather, they are meant to be considered in combination or in totality to tell a story about the business. In doing so, numbers actually present the strength and competitive advantage of the business over its competitors.

Summary

- Over three to five years, a growth company should possess:
  - Revenue > 15%
  - Net Profit > 15%
  - Cash Flow > 15%
  - Net Profit Margin > 8%
  - Return on Equity > 15%
  - Debt to Equity < 0.5
  - Cash Ratio > 0.5
  - Dividend Payout Ratio: 15%–50%
  - CAPEX Ratio < 80%
  - Positive Free Cash Flow
- The above numbers serve as a rule of thumb.
- Consistency is key when comparing the numbers over the past five years.

CHAPTER 7

Valuation—The Fourth Piece of the Puzzle

The Valuation of a Stock

The fourth and final piece of the puzzle is *valuation*—the financial projection. This is the most important piece to access once the other three pieces have been addressed. Here, valuation is what we call the final part of assessment before buying into a stock. Needless to say, every stock has a price tag. So, at what price is a stock considered cheap? This chapter serves to answer this question.

Though we cannot expect to buy a stock at its absolute bottom, for example, in the 2008–09 crash, when the Straits Times Index

(STI) was at its lowest, at 1,500 points, and sell it at its peak in 2010, when the STI had recovered to above 3,300 points, we can avoid doing the opposite. Many investors commit the mistake of buying high, when someone they know is supposedly making a killing in the stock market, and selling low, when prices start to dive. Now that you are aware that Mr. Market is subject to mood swings, you need to know how to make full use of its irrationality, in order to purchase stocks at bargain prices and sell when others are ready to pay a premium price. In order to do this, you need to know how to calculate the intrinsic value of the company based on a certain set of assumptions. Valuation can help you achieve this, so that you can buy a growth company when it is trading at a discount from its intrinsic value.

In relation to the valuation of a stock, there are three types of valuation methods that we often use to determine growth companies:

1. Price-to-Earnings Ratio (PE Ratio)
2. Price-to-Earnings to Growth Rate Ratio (PEG Ratio)
3. Discounted Earning Model

Now let us go through these valuation methods one by one.

Why Earnings Are Used

When valuing a growth company, it is best to use a metric like earnings per share instead of operation cash flow. This is because growth companies tend to spend more on development costs to expand their businesses further, causing the operation's cash flow to be plowed back into the business. However, some companies are good at manipulating earnings when they do business on credit with debtors. Such manipulation is short term. In the long run, the company's true colors should reveal themselves. To ensure that we have an accurate assessment of a company, it is important for us to obtain a track record that goes back a minimum of three to five years. Healthy numbers reported in the past do not imply that a company will stay healthy into the future. However, such figures are definitely easier to interpret and project into the future, as compared to a company that reports inconsistency in its revenue, net profit, and cash flow. This inconsistency makes it extremely hard to value or project the company into the future when determining its intrinsic value. Again, consistency is a key quality when comparing these numbers.

Price-to-Earnings Ratio

Price-to-earnings ratio, or PE ratio for short, is among the three indicators that we use to gauge whether a growth company is undervalued or overvalued. The formula is:

$$\text{Price to Earnings (PE)} = \frac{\text{Share price}}{\text{Earnings per share}}$$

Say, for example, a company had earnings per share (EPS) of $2 in 2010. On 30 June 2011, the share price was valued by the market at $10. To obtain the PE ratio, we take $10 divided by $2. This will give us a PE ratio of 5 ($10 ÷ $2) for 2010 earnings. This PE ratio can tell us two things:

1. Assuming all things are constant, the number of years needed for investors to get back their initial investment. If the PE ratio is 5, it will take five years for investors to earn back their initial investment of $10. (This is only true in theory. In reality, however, earnings dynamics can change materially.)
2. The price that investors are willing to pay for every dollar of earning in the company. If the PE ratio is 5, it means an investor is willing to pay $5 for every $1 of EPS.

Generally, the PE ratio reflects how optimistic the market is concerning the growth of a company. Growth investors are more willing to pay a premium price for a company with a high PE ratio, which might lead them into a growth trap if the expansion plan were unsuccessful.

In the first quarter of 2011, Q&M Dental was trading at S$0.60 a share with EPS of S$0.0146 in 2010. With this information, the PE ratio worked out to be above 40 times 2010 earnings! In this case, investors are more willing to pay for a promising business like Q&M Dental, where the management intends to extend its dental services business into the China market. With a PE ratio of 40, it suggests that investors are paying S$40 for every S$1 of earnings. This might sound ridiculous to you, but the expectation of the market is so strong that most investors ignore the basic fundamentals here. Although there might be scalability in Q&M's expansion into overseas markets, which would push revenue and earnings up in future, a high PE means that investors have nearly zero protection against any downside risks. In our opinion, it is better for us to disregard the irrationality of the market and avoid joining the crowd just because a share price has increased.

Generally, high-PE stocks are dangerous. For instance, in 2010, Company A and B from the same industry have a PE ratio of 10 and 30, respectively. As the ratios suggest, investors are bullish about Company B, because they are willing to pay three times more than they would for Company A. This says that Company B is a higher expectation stocks to the investors. However, such confidence would be misplaced if the new earnings do not meet the growth investors' expectations. As a result, the stock falls behind that of Company A. Between the two, it can be said that Company A is a safer choice, because investors have lower expectations. As such, any negative announcements made by the company are not likely to bring the company's share price any lower, since there is less room to fall further. Conversely, any slight improvement in earnings of a low-PE company will likely draw interest among investors, who will purchase the stock and push its share price up to new heights! As a guide, a stock that has a PE ratio less than 10 is said to have a higher margin of safety than those with a high PE ratio (e.g., >20).

However, valuation using PE ratio is a double-edged sword because a low PE does not mean that the company is undervalued. For instance, the market may think that the company is heading into a time of turbulence, and that is why it is low. On the other hand, a high PE ratio might not mean that the company is overvalued. Reasons are:

1. It may be in a cyclical industry.
2. It has exceptional items.

First, good growth companies should be able to withstand a downturn and either maintain or increase their earnings and revenue at a rate of more than 15 percent over a period of five years. They should be able to provide hard evidence of sustainability and consistency from their past records. If a company is inconsistent in its earnings, then it is likely to be considered a cyclical company (e.g., shipping, construction). If you use PE ratio as a valuation tool for cyclical companies, as illustrated in Figure 7.1, you may find that the PE ratio will show an opposite result. In other words, during good times, these companies will have a lower PE ratio due to higher earnings and

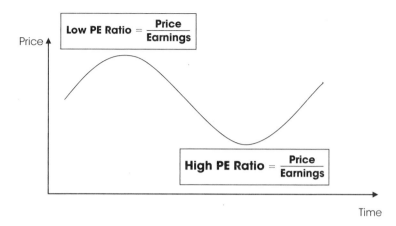

Figure 7.1   PE ratio of a cyclical company

better prospects. However, during a downturn, the PE ratio will be grossly high because of lower earnings or it may be nearly impossible to calculate due to losses when the economy is at its bottom.

In this case, a low PE ratio can be misleading if you are to think that it is an undervalued stock.

Here, a gain or loss of exceptional items will cause a low and high PE ratio, respectively. Thus, it is important to exclude such items when calculating a company's PE ratio. By comparing a company's PE ratio with the industry average and that of competitors, it may reveal whether a company is a better buy.

There are investors who solely rely on the comparison of PE ratio to judge whether a company is undervalued. In our opinion, a comparison of PE ratio without reading the fine lines in company financial statements can be very risky. Imagine that a good growth company, one that has been performing very well for 10 years with a PE ratio of around 15, is hit by a temporary problem or carries an exceptional item that causes the PE ratio to rise above 40x. This hike in PE ratio could lead you to have a false perception of the company's valuation. Upon comparison with an average company that has a PE ratio of 18, you will end up buying a lousy business at a higher price when the affected company returns to its normal earnings. So, when using the PE ratio, you must ensure the company is a growth company with consistency in earnings.

Types of PE Ratio

There are three types of PE ratio that most investors and analysts use:

1. Historical PE—based on annual earnings
   Historical data is based on the current price divided by earnings from the previous financial year. As it is based on earnings that have already been achieved, it is a useful point for us to start with. Normally, investors can find the historical earnings in the company's latest annual report. For instance, in its 2009 annual report, Japan Food had earnings of $0.0357 per share. In the first quarter of 2010, the company was trading at $0.23. Therefore, its historical PE ratio is 6.4 ($0.23 ÷ $0.0357). In this case, this is useful when the company has just released its annual result for a financial year and before the release of the next quarter result. If you want to use the results from the latest quarter to calculate PE ratio, you must use trailing PE to gain a more accurate assessment.
2. Trailing PE—based on recent four quarters earnings
   Trailing PE is more current than historical PE because it uses current price divided by the company's results in the past four quarters. For instance, the sum of the recent four quarters is 2009Q4 + 2010Q1 + 2010Q2 + 2010Q3. We use the results from the latest four quarters when we are in the year end of 2010.
3. Forward PE—Use annual data two to three years ahead from broker forecasts
   This is based on estimated earnings obtained by analysts. Here, we take the current share price divided by estimated earnings, which is derived through projections at a certain percentage into the next four quarters. In short, the earnings are merely forecasts into the near future. It must be said that this approach is more risky. After all, no one knows what will happen tomorrow.

We will concentrate on historical PE and trailing PE only because these are based on real results and provide some form of benchmarking. Remember to look for growth companies that have a PE ratio of below 10, as that often means that the stock is undervalued.

Last but not least, research has shown that if you invest in low-PE-ratio stocks in the long run, they will outperform stocks that have a high PE ratio. For instance, in 2003, the PE ratio for SMRT, a transport operator company, was 12.5, while Armstrong, a precision engineering company, had a PE ratio of 7. If you compare the growth between these two companies until 2010, SMRT's stock price had an average compound of 19 percent annually, while Armstrong had an average compound of 29 percent annually. Here, the general rule is the lower the PE, the cheaper the stock. However, be wary of companies that have a very ultra-low PE ratio, say less than five times. Interpreting the PE ratio can be a challenge if you do not consider a company's growth rate. In relation to this, some stocks might reflect a very low PE but experience no growth, therein becoming value trap stocks. This leads us to the next equation—price-to-earnings-to-growth (PEG) ratio.

Price-to-Earnings-to-Growth Ratio

PEG ratio is one of the most important criteria for valuation when looking into growth companies. It calculates the PE ratio of a stock in comparison to the growth rate. Introduced by Peter Lynch, the PEG ratio is a fast and accurate indicator by which to determine whether a company is overvalued or undervalued. If a sector of all companies has the same growth rate and risk, then using the PE ratio to gauge the value of the company would be fine. Unfortunately, companies in similar sectors grow at different rates. The PEG ratio shows a more complete picture, as compared to just using the PE ratio, since many low-PE-ratio stocks are cheap and rightfully so. In these cases, these stocks are cheap as the business has no growth potential. As an investor, there is certainly no point in buying companies that do not have growth potential.

As an investor, there is certainly no point in buying companies that do not have growth potential.

Here, the formula for PEG ratio is:

$$PEG = \frac{PE\ Ratio}{Compound\ Annual\ Growth\ Rate}$$

For instance, if the company is trading at a PE ratio of 30, we want to ensure that the company is growing at a rate of 30 percent per annum to compensate for this high PE, which makes the PEG 1 (30 ÷ 30). For investors, the growth of companies is calculated based on the EPS of the companies. Future growth rate is unpredictable, as no one can predict what the future earnings of a company will be, but we can have a better picture of the company when using its historical growth rate, because successful companies always leave a good trail behind. In this case, we want to find out the company's growth rate over the past five years.

For example, Company A has a PE ratio of 25 with a growth rate of 15 percent. It will have a PEG ratio of 1.6 (25 ÷ 15). Company B, on the other hand, has a PE ratio of 35 and a growth rate of 50 percent. It will have a PEG ratio of 0.7 (35 ÷ 50). In this case, Company B is considered a better bargain, even though it has a PE ratio of 35. Using the PEG ratio, where a company's growth rate is taken into consideration, shows that Company B has more room to grow.

Determining the Rate of Growth-Compounded Annual Growth Rate (CAGR)

Compound annual growth rate (CAGR) is an average growth rate over a period of several years. Here, three key variables can be used to determine the compounded growth rate—revenue, net profit, and operational cash flow. The formula for CAGR is as follows:

$$CAGR = (FV \div PV) \, 1 \div n - 1$$

FV = Future Value (Final-Year EPS or Revenue)
PV = Present Value (First-Year EPS or Revenue)
n = Number of years

As shown in Table 7.1, if the company's EPS in 2005 and 2009 was 0.02 and 0.10 respectively, then the CAGR of its EPS is 49.5% [(0.10 ÷ 0.02) 1 ÷ 4 - 1]. Here, we define growth companies as ones that grow at more than 15 percent compounded consistently.

Table 7.1   Computation of CAGR

Year	Earnings per Share
2005 (PV)	0.02
2006	0.03
2007	0.05
2008	0.08
2009 (FV)	0.10
CAGR	49.5%

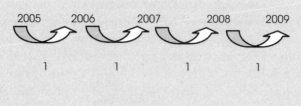

n = 4 (1+1+1+1)

Anything less than that would be considered a nongrowth company. Although no historical data is a substitute for a forecast, CAGR over a number of years (e.g., last five years) is a better indication of a trend than a single year's growth, which may be misleading at times. That is why we want to obtain a track record of a minimum of three to five years.

To be more conservative when calculating the growth rate of a company, we will halve the calculated growth rate. In this case, we will take the growth rate to be around 25 percent instead of 49.5 percent. Hence, if the PE ratio is 10 and the growth rate is 25 percent, the resultant PEG ratio is 0.4. This ratio shows that the company is undervalued. The other key point to note is that when calculating a company's growth rate, past growth rates cannot be taken as projections for future growth rates. Growth trends tend to change in the future. Owing to such rises and falls in growth trends, it is very important for us to determine the growth factors based on both the business and management aspect of the company (first and second pieces of the puzzle), by looking at expansion plans and possible room for expansion. Based on our experience, when calculating PEG ratio, it is better to be safe than sorry by limiting the growth rate to less than 20 percent, even if the business looks promising (e.g., >30 percent).

When calculating PEG ratio, it is better to be safe than sorry by limiting the growth rate to less than 20 percent.

Table 7.2 Relationship between PEG Ratio and valuation

PEG Ratio (x)	Valuation
<0.5	Undervalue
0.5–1	Fair Value
>1	Avoid/SELL
>2	SELL

In terms of margin of safety, refer to Table 7.2. When the PEG ratio is 1x, the valuation of a stock is considered fair value. But when it is half of the growth rate, it is considered undervalued (margin of safety 50 percent). This means that you are paying a discount to its future growth. If it is more than 1x, we assume that is overvalued because the PE ratio is twice the growth rate, which is a sell signal, because the PEG is 2x. This is one of the best tools for calculating growth companies to see whether it is selling at a bargain price. So when the PEG ratio is 2x, would you still buy it? You will most certainly have to think twice now!

Although PEG ratio makes it simple to find undervalued companies, you must know that it also has its limitations. First, it can only be used to gauge small-growth companies. When it comes to mature companies with low growth, PEG ratio will become ineffective, as it would appear to be overvalued when calculated. Second, it can only be used on companies that have a consistent growth in their EPS. In other words, you will not be able to use the PEG ratio for companies with a cyclical nature. The use of PEG ratio is also rather limited when you use it on a company that has declining growth.

From Table 7.3, assuming the growth rates across the four companies to be the same, Company A, with a PEG of 0.5x, is said to be undervalued. Company B, with a PEG ratio of 1, is said to be of fair

Table 7.3 Relationship between PE ratio, earnings growth rate, and PEG ratio in four companies

	Company A	Company B	Company C	Company D
PE Ratio (x)	5	10	15	20
Earnings Growth Rate	10%	10%	10%	10%
PEG Ratio (x)	0.5	1	1.5	2

value. Meanwhile, Companies C and D are considered overvalued since they have a PEG ratio of 1.5 and 2, respectively. As a general rule, the best time to acquire an outstanding business is when the PEG ratio is less than 0.5. In short, the lower the PEG, the cheaper the stock is.

Discounted Earnings Model

The third method of valuation is the discounted earnings model. This model of valuation was described by John Burr Williams in his classic book, *The Theory of Investment Value*. Using this approach, we are ready to project the future earnings of a company, once we have reasonable confidence in a company's business. Here, the main objective is to find out how much the company is worth—its intrinsic value—and calculate a reasonable margin of safety.

Intrinsic Value

Intrinsic value is defined as the total amount of cash that can be taken out of a company in its lifetime, discounted at the present worth at an appropriate interest rate. Put simply, it suggests the true value of the company, or the present value of a company's accumulated earnings, over few years.

It can be calculated using different valuation approaches, such as the discounted earning model, discounted cash-flow model, and discounted dividend model. Intrinsic value is calculated based on an estimation of the projected growth of a company. Therefore, every individual is entitled to their independent perspective when estimating how much a company could grow in the future (e.g., 10 years later), based on its current earnings. In addition, there would be no permanently correct estimation for growth, as the amount varies from person to person. If anything, intrinsic value is dependent on the individual's risk appetite.

A parallel scenario to the above would be, say, an analyst working in a value fund firm who shares with us that different analysts have different valuation approaches. Regardless of the approach adopted, each analyst has generated positive growth in the fund; they all are able to achieve multi-bagger returns. Here, in determining a company's valuation, our main goal is really to find companies that are said to be worth $1, for example, but that we can buy at $0.50 and sell at $1 or more.

Table 7.4   Financial background of Company A

Company	A
Current Year	2010
EPS (2010)	S$0.073
EPS CAGR (2005–2010)	20%
Current Share Price	S$0.50

Generally, the discounted cash-flow model is used for blue-chip or mature companies, such as Singapore Press Holding (SPH) and Singapore Airport Terminal Services (SATS). As these companies are more stable, they have a strong generation of free cash flow every year. Since growth companies require more capital to be injected back into the business to grow and expand further, they tend to have higher capital expenditures. This will affect the volume of free cash flow (FCF) during the initial stages. As such, the discounted earnings model will be useful when it comes to evaluating the intrinsic value of growth companies.

There is a methodological approach for us to arrive at an estimation of a company's intrinsic value. From Table 7.4, let us compute the intrinsic value of Company A using three simple steps.

Step 1: Choose the Projection Growth Rate   Imagine the EPS for the current year (2010) amounts to $0.073. Based on its historical growth rate, Company A has been growing at 20 percent from 2005 to 2010, which is five years of its earnings track record. Based on this piece of information, to project the historical growth rate, in our opinion, will be too optimistic; you do not want to end up entering at a high price because the projected earnings are ridiculously high and end up in a growth trap if the earnings are not fulfilled in the next 10 years. As such, it is better for us to be more conservative. In this case, we assume Company A will continue to grow its EPS, but at a slower rate of 10 percent, or half the original growth rate and with a company lifetime of time years (lifetime could be more than that). Even at this conservative rate, value-growth investors will be able to find growth companies selling below their intrinsic value. In this case, the EPS stands at $0.08 (rounded to two decimal places) in 2011. Table 7.5 shows 10 years of forecast earnings, assuming that the business is still around and profitable.

Table 7.5   EPS of Company A from 2011 to 2020

	2011	2012	2013	2014	2015	2016	2017	2018	2019	2020
EPS	0.080	0.088	0.097	0.106	0.117	0.129	0.142	0.156	0.171	0.189

In this case, it would not have been possible for you to determine whether a business will still be around in the next 10 years, if you do not already understand the company's business. To determine a business's sustainability, you must first be able to envision the business's place in the market in the future. If you are unable to do so, for whatever reason, you should avoid this company altogether. For this reason, companies in the high-tech industry are often avoided, as it can be very difficult to estimate their value, as a result of steep competition within the industry.

Step 2: Discounting Risk-Free Interest Rate   The forecast earnings for the next 10 years must be discounted back to determine the company's present value. Why is that so?

A dollar today has greater value than a dollar next year. If inflation is at 4 percent, S$1 next year will be worth S$0.96 of a dollar today. Surely your parents must have been telling you this, in principle, for some time now. Over the years, they must have boasted about the number of things that they could have bought with a SGDS$1 coin 10 years ago, as compared to today. Here, what they mean is that the money value has depreciated with time. In view of the effects of inflation, the future value of S$1 must be discounted to the present value. Since we are providing a forecast for up to 10 years, it is important for us to determine the future value based on the present value.

So, what is the percentage we should use to discount future value? Theoretically, many investors use the *risk-free interest rate*. It is a rate of return for any investment with zero risk. In this case, investors want to have a benchmark when comparing a stock that could promise a higher return. In the United States, the risk-free interest rate can be approximated based on the rate of U.S. Treasury bills, since they typically pose a very small risk. In Singapore, a risk-free investment would be Central Provident Fund (CPF) special or retirement account, which could yield up to a 4 percent return. In other words, if you were to put S$10,000 in a CPF special account, you are guaranteed two things: You will earn 4 percent compounded interest annually and, so, when it matures (or when you retire), you are guaranteed an amount of S$10,000 back. Thus, if you have an investment that gives a return of 1 or 2 percent per year, it would be better off to place the money in your CPF account and let it compound at a rate of 4 percent.

Here, the rate is pegged to the 12-month average yield of 10-year Singapore Government Securities (10YSGS) plus 1 or 4 percent, whichever is higher (adjusted quarterly). Due to fluctuations in the rate, investors should regularly check updates of the rate, which can be obtained from the CPF board, if they want to invest in the Singapore stock market.

The formula for the discount factor (DF) is $1 \div (1 + \text{Risk-Free Interest Rate})^n$, where n is the number of years. In the first year, the DF is $1 \div (1+0.04)^1$ assuming a risk-free rate of 4 percent (refer to Table 7.6). For the subsequent year, 2012, the result will be $1 \div (1+0.04)^2$ and so on.

Here, Table 7.7 provides a breakdown of the adjusted DF in relation to the risk-free rate.

Do note that risk-free rates in Table 7.7 should be adjusted when CPF's interest rates change. In the event that government bonds offer a 5 percent interest rate in the future, it is also advisable to peg

Table 7.6   DF based on a risk-free rate of 4 percent

	2011	2012	2013	2014	2015	2016	2017	2018	2019	2020
DF	0.962	0.925	0.889	0.855	0.822	0.790	0.760	0.731	0.703	0.676

Table 7.7   Breakdown of adjusted DF in relation to the risk-free rate

Risk-Free Rate	Year 1	Year 2	Year 3	Year 4	Year 5	Year 6	Year 7	Year 8	Year 9	Year 10
1%	0.990	0.980	0.971	0.961	0.951	0.942	0.933	0.923	0.914	0.905
2%	0.980	0.961	0.942	0.924	0.906	0.888	0.871	0.853	0.837	0.820
3%	0.971	0.943	0.915	0.888	0.863	0.837	0.813	0.789	0.766	0.744
4%	0.962	0.925	0.889	0.855	0.822	0.790	0.760	0.731	0.703	0.676
5%	0.952	0.907	0.864	0.823	0.784	0.746	0.711	0.677	0.645	0.614
6%	0.943	0.890	0.840	0.792	0.747	0.705	0.665	0.627	0.592	0.558
7%	0.935	0.873	0.816	0.763	0.713	0.666	0.623	0.582	0.544	0.508
8%	0.926	0.857	0.794	0.735	0.681	0.630	0.583	0.540	0.500	0.463
9%	0.917	0.842	0.772	0.708	0.650	0.596	0.547	0.502	0.460	0.422
10%	0.909	0.826	0.751	0.683	0.621	0.564	0.513	0.467	0.424	0.386

the interest rate accordingly, being at 5 percent when calculating the intrinsic value. This adjustment is reflected in Table 7.8.

Back to calculating the growth of $0.073 at 10 percent per annum, using a risk-free rate of 4 percent, we will also determine the discounted value (DV) of its future earnings.

To determine discounted value, multiply projected EPS with DF. For instance, by referring to Table 7.9, EPS in 2011 is estimated at $0.08. By multiplying its DF of 0.962, the DV is $0.077. That tells us the present value of 2011 EPS.

From Table 7.9, the present value for EPS is $0.128 (more accurate), instead of $0.189, in 2020.

Step 3: Adding the Discounted Earnings to Obtain the Intrinsic Value The intrinsic value is obtained when you add up the discounted value of EPS for the 10 years – accumulated earnings over period of 10 years.

For example, as shown in Table 7.10, the intrinsic value calculated for Company A is $1.007 (estimated at $1). So, if the current

Table 7.8 DF when interest rate is pegged at 5 percent

	2011	2012	2013	2014	2015	2016	2017	2018	2019	2020
DF	0.952	0.907	0.864	0.823	0.784	0.746	0.711	0.677	0.645	0.614

Table 7.9 DV based on a risk-free rate of 4 percent

	2011	2012	2013	2014	2015	2016	2017	2018	2019	2020
EPS	0.080	0.088	0.097	0.106	0.117	0.129	0.142	0.156	0.171	0.189
DF	0.962	0.925	0.889	0.855	0.822	0.790	0.760	0.731	0.703	0.676
DV	0.077	0.082	0.086	0.091	0.097	0.102	0.108	0.114	0.121	0.128

Table 7.10 Intrinsic Value after adding up the discounted value of EPS for the 10 years

	2011	2012	2013	2014	2015	2016	2017	2018	2019	2020
EPS	0.080	0.088	0.097	0.106	0.117	0.129	0.142	0.156	0.171	0.189
DF	0.962	0.925	0.889	0.855	0.822	0.790	0.760	0.731	0.703	0.676
DV	0.077	0.082	0.086	0.091	0.097	0.102	0.108	0.114	0.121	0.128
Intrinsic Value	S$ 1.007									

share price is priced at $0.50, would you buy when you know that its real value will be estimated at $1 in the next 10 years? The answer is pretty obvious. In this case, Company A is selling at a discounted price. The stock is undervalued, and you should not hesitate to buy when the opportunity comes.

However, the calculation of intrinsic value only provides an estimated number for reference. To support your decision, you may want to obtain a different metric based on different sets of assumptions. For instance, you might assume that there is no growth in this company because you understand the company inside out. Or the EPS amount might have been worked out with the exclusion of some profit being added back. If you had done so, you would have obtained a different intrinsic value. Nevertheless, with this information, you can make you own decision as to whether to buy this business or simply walk away, especially when the company is quoting us a price that is higher than its intrinsic value.

As there are a lot of estimates involved in our calculation of intrinsic value, it is best to understand the first three pieces of the puzzle. In this case, projected growth rates should not rely solely on past growth rates, but also factor in the quality of the business, management, and financial numbers. The more positive the qualitative analysis—say, the business has strong moats and its management has initiated an expansion plan—the growth rate can be estimated at a higher rate (keep at 20 percent), as compared to a management team without much of a plan. This will not only give you more confidence in holding that particular stock but will also provide you with a more precise assumption, because you believe it will generate more profit and cash in future.

For instance, we are likely to provide a higher projected growth rate for Company A compared to Company B, because the management team in Company A has announced plans to open 20 new outlets in five years (Table 7.11). This is an addition of 15 outlets compared to

Table 7.11   Projected growth rate for Company A and Company B

Company	Existing outlets	New outlets (5 years later)	Total outlets (5 years later)	Projected growth rate
A	10	20	30	31.6%
B	10	5	15	10.6%

Company B. Let us assume that both companies are in the same industry and have the same average outlet sales and net profit.

In Singapore, this is why a growth company like Q&M Dental tends to trade at a value that is many times its earnings.

When assuming the growth rate of a company, it largely depends on the risk appetite of investors. The higher you project the future growth in the next 10 years, the higher will be the intrinsic value obtained. When you consider an intrinsic value to be high, you are also accepting the risk of paying for something at a higher price. Figure 7.2 serves as a quick guide to risk level. Therefore, just like PEG ratio, it is best to keep your estimated growth rate at 20 percent or less, to be conservative. You should use a projected growth rate of 10 to 20 percent only when you think that a company's expansion plan is going to work out very well from the standpoint of scaling the business operation overseas or in current markets. Sometimes it is advisable to project the company at 0 percent growth. This is often useful during a recession. You will discover that, even at 0 percent, you will be able to filter out undervalued companies. When investing during a crisis period, you will then be able to scoop up reasonable undervalued stocks.

Now we understand why Warren Buffett likes to invest in a business that is easy to understand, managed by honest and trusted managers; it is a lot easier to project the future earnings and cash flows of such businesses. Here, value-growth investors should also look out for companies that can continue to increase its intrinsic value to reward them. Such companies will be rewarded by an increase in price in the long run. However, not all investments will continue to rise. Some will fall—this is when the intrinsic value starts to drop year after year after an investor had acquired a particular stock. It starts to decline due to a drop in the company's earnings. In this case, holding a stock that continues to deteriorate is known as a *value trap*. While it is impossible to avoid this, it is

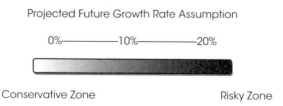

Figure 7.2 Projected future growth rate and subjected risk

possible to cut your losses by doing your homework and confirming that the drop is permanent. In doing so, you are also unlikely to pay for a price that is higher than the intrinsic value, thus, further limiting the risk that you are subjected to.

Margin of Safety

Knowing how to compute intrinsic value is just the beginning of valuing a company. You will be able to appreciate intrinsic value more accurately only when it is deducted from the market price to determine its margin of safety. Such is the importance of the margin of safety—being the three most important words in investing—that Ben Graham devoted an entire chapter to highlight its importance in his book *The Intelligent Investor*. In which case, it will be more effective if you have incorporated the concept of margin of safety into evaluating a company's intrinsic value.

Warren Buffett likes to invest in a business that is easy to understand, managed by honest and trusted managers; it is a lot easier to project the future cash flows of such businesses.

Having a margin of safety does not guarantee a successful investment, but it takes care of downside to minimize errors. It helps to eliminate capital losses or reduce investment risks. In other words, when you have a margin of safety, it will serve as a buffer for any investment and leave room for errors in the event that wrong assumptions were made during the period of valuing a stock.

Remember, capital preservation is the first rule in investing. When it comes to money, we expect positive returns. Before thinking of capital appreciation in the stock market, value-growth investors must think about capital preservation first. We invest only when the risk is reduced to its minimum (e.g., no debt). In the outside world, we pay for personal, home, and car insurance policies to cover our losses in the event of catastrophic events (e.g., fire, accident, or personal injury). In investing, we also need to have good protection for our investments—a margin of safety. The wider the margin, the more protection we will have.

In investing, we also need to have a good protection for our investments—a margin of safety. The wider the margin, the more protection we will have.

For instance, Investor A, being more bullish about a growth business, uses a growth rate of 10 percent to calculate a company's intrinsic value. Investor B, being more conservative about the future growth of a similar company, might use 0 percent growth to determine its intrinsic value. Needless to say, the two investors will obtain a different intrinsic value of the same company. But, with a margin of safety, the success of both investors in investing is not dependent on the exact intrinsic value; the margin of safety serves as better protection against wrong assumptions. In relation to this, a margin of safety is affected by intrinsic value and the market price. When the intrinsic value and share price of a company change, the margin of safety will change.

$$\text{Margin of Safety} = \frac{\text{Intrinsic Value} - \text{Share Price}}{\text{Intrinsic Value}} \times 100\%$$

The following are three most important terms when using margin of safety.

Undervalued

In general, a company with an intrinsic value of $1 is considered a good buffer when you buy it at the price of $0.50. This gives a margin of safety equivalent to 50 percent.

$$\text{Margin of Safety} = \frac{\text{Intrinsic Value} - \text{Share Price}}{\text{Intrinsic Value}} \times 100\%$$

$$= \frac{\$1 - \$0.50}{\$1} \times 100\%$$

$$= 50\%$$

Fair Value

When the stock trades at $1, it is trading at fair value.

$$\text{Margin of Safety} = \frac{\text{Intrinsic Value} - \text{Share Price}}{\text{Intrinsic Value}} \times 100\%$$

$$= \frac{\$1 - \$1}{\$1} \times 100\%$$

$$= 0\%$$

Overvalued

If the same stock has an intrinsic value of $1, it is considered over-valued when bought at the price of $1.50.

This will provide a margin of safety equivalent to −50%.

$$\text{Margin of Safety} = \frac{\text{Intrinsic Value} - \text{Share Price}}{\text{Intrinsic Value}} \times 100\%$$

$$= \frac{\$1 - \$1.50}{\$1} \times 100\%$$

$$= -50\%$$

As it is, there is no hard-and-fast rule regarding how much margin of safety needs to be in place in order for you to become a prudent investor. Obviously, a 50 percent margin of safety will generally be better than paying a fair price (0 percent margin of safety) for the same company. The wider the margin of safety, the better you will be protected should a financial crisis hit, or when you make a wrong assumption.

Table 7.12 is a good start for determining the margin of safety required. However, there are companies, like blue-chip compa-nies, that are unlikely to sell at a bargain price with a margin of safety of more than 50 percent. Since most blue-chip companies are not growth companies, they will normally trade at a fair price or even be overvalued, rather than being priced at a bargain price, even during times of crisis. This fits the bill of one of the Warren Buffett's statements about quality companies: "It's far better to buy a wonderful company at a fair price than a fair company at a won-derful price."

Table 7.12   Relationship between margin of safety and a company's valuation

Margin of Safety	Valuation
> 50%	Undervalued
50%–0%	Slightly Undervalued–Fair Value
>–10%	Fair Value–Overvalued
>–50%	Grossly Overvalued

Margin of Safety—A More In-Depth Analysis

When investors buy into a company, they are not buying only the stock but also are effectively buying the whole of the company's assets, cash, and even debts. Some companies have net cash in their financial statement (total cash − total borrowing). Some also have net debts in their financial statements. With this, we would have a greater margin of safety if the company has more cash than debt. Conversely, we would have a low margin of safety if it has more debt than cash. We will increase the margin if we are paying cash in return for a positive cash flow and reduce our margin of safety if we are paying cash in return for helping the company pay off its debt. The formula for margin of safety is:

$$\frac{\text{Intrinsic Value} - \text{Share Price} - (\text{Cash per Share} - \text{Debt per Share})}{\text{Intrinsic Value}} \times 100\%$$

For instance, let us say that a company has net cash. It has cash of $0.20 per share and debt of $0.10 per share. This will result in a net cash (cash per share − debt per share) value of $0.10 ($0.20 − $0.10).

$$\frac{\$1 - (\$0.50 - \$0.10)}{\$1} \times 100\% = 60\%$$

Now let us look at a company with net debt. It has cash of $0.10 per share and debt of $0.20 per share. This will result in a net debt of $0.10 ($0.20 − $0.10).

$$\frac{\$1 - (\$0.50 - \$0.10)}{\$1} \times 100\% = 40\%$$

From the above, our margin of safety increases to 60 percent, as we take into consideration net cash. However, if the company has net debt, our margin of safety will be reduced to 40 percent.

The best time to have a great margin of safety is when the market is depressed or when a company is heavily punished by the market due to bad news. For instance, on May 7, 2010, Design Studio was summoned to court by Talal Saeed Ghazi (a Dubai company). The claim amounted to S$115.2 million. If Design Studio

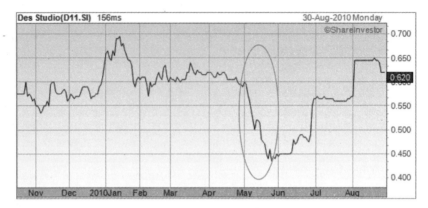

Figure 7.3   Design Studio 1-Year Historical Price
Source: www.shareinvestor.com

had lost this lawsuit, the company might face bankruptcy, requiring it to issue additional new shares to finance debts or to take out a big loan from the bank. In this instance, Mr. Market was in great fear, and the share price dropped from S$0.60 to S$0.45 within a month.

In Figure 7.3, it can be seen that the price of Design Studio took a sharp plunge. Since everyone became fearful and started to sell their shares, we took the opportunity to buy its stocks at S$0.45. We consider ourselves blessed to have entered at this price because, a week later, the price rebounded.

> The market is there to serve us and not to guide us.
>
> —*Ben Graham*

Remember, as stated by Ben Graham, the market is there to serve us and not to guide us. During the financial crisis of 2008–2009, a growth company such as Boustead was trading at its low of S$0.45 in the first quarter of 2009, when its intrinsic value stood at S$1.60 at 0 percent growth rate, which gave us a good margin of safety of 71.8 percent. During the same period, Hsu Fu Chi was trading at below S$0.30, with an intrinsic value of S$1.10 and a 0 percent growth rate, as determined using a risk-free rate of 4 percent (excluding the China risk rate). That gave us a margin of safety of 70 percent. There were additional companies that were selling at bargain prices. If we were to mention them all, this book would be much thicker.

However, during this period, average investors would not dare to enter the stock market, for fear that prices would continue to drop. One key lesson to learn here, as a value-growth investor, is that you should take such a period as an opportunity to scoop up bargain stocks. Remember, thinking as a contrarian will help make you a successful investor—be greedy when others are fearful! Most of the time, the market, in a state of fear, does not reflect the share price of its intrinsic value. Understandably, it can be very difficult to make a purchase when the investment mood and environment are shrouded with negativity. Investors who can overcome this and take action regardless of market pessimism will definitely become very successful. The main objective of this chapter is to teach you how to buy growth companies at a low price (undervalued) and sell them (if you intend to) when the price is higher or overvalued. On top of that, avoid buying a stock when it is overvalued (e.g., negative margin of safety). Though financial projection is not very reliable, it is still better than any other forms of prediction. In relation to this, Warren Buffett once said, "It is better to be approximately right than precisely wrong."

A word of caution: This section, "Valuation of a Stock," should be used only to determine *when* investors want to enter or exit stock market. It should not be used to determine the quality of the stock. The price is mainly based on market sentiments and not the quality of the stock.

During the 2008–09 crisis, some growth companies did not continue to grow after the price correction, owing to the respective growth factors of companies. Thus, the next chapter is dedicated to considering the growth factors of companies, so that we can obtain a clearer picture of value-growth investing. In doing so, we can make a decision based on a complete Jigsaw Puzzle Model rather than based on bits and pieces of information. Together with the three other puzzle pieces—business, management, and numbers—you will be better equipped to make an investment decision on whether to buy, monitor, or sell a stock with greater confidence. However, prior to buying, remember to learn how to screen a stock first.

Summary

The following table serves as a guide to time the buying and selling of a stock based on its valuation.

Action	Valuation	PE Ratio	PEG Ratio	Intrinsic Value Margin of Safety
BUY	Undervalued	< 5	< 0.5	> 50%
BUY/HOLD	Fair Value	5–10	0.5–1	50%–0%
SELL/HOLD	Fair Value–Overvalued	>15	>1	>–10%
SELL	Grossly Overvalued	>20	>2	>–50%

8

Screening—Buy— Monitor—Sell

Screening (Using Numbers against Competitors)

To get you started on finding growth companies, you can begin by looking at the financial numbers (we will get back to the qualitative side of our analysis once a company passes this screening stage). As you should understand by now, financial numbers are one of the most important sources of information when it comes to value investing. In this case, these numbers are capable of telling us a story of a company, indicate its financial performance, or even the strength of moats used by the business. They also serve as an indicator as to how sustainable a business is. Therefore, when screening growth companies, you can start by looking at the right financial numbers. To help you do this, we are going to show the step-by-step process used to screen these numbers, all for the purpose of comparing a company with its competitors.

To start this screening process, for example, we will choose an easy-to-understand industry, such as the food and beverage (F&B) industry. We will start by comparing four companies in this industry to keep things simple. They are listed in the Singapore Exchange (SGX): BreadTalk Group Limited, ABR Holdings Limited, Sakae Holding Limited, and Tung Lok Restaurant Limited.

Here, this screening process will be broken down into five stages. Companies that pass Stage 1 of the screening process will proceed to Stage 2, and so on. If a company does not pass Stage 1, it will be eliminated. Once you have learned this process, you may want to use this process for a selection of companies that is within your circle of competence, as you are more likely to be familiar with the competitors of a specific company. Using this process, you are more likely to obtain a detailed picture of which company is better.

Stage 1: Consistency in Key Performance Indicators

At this stage, we are looking for consistent growth in the key performance indicators, which are revenue, profit after tax, and net operational cash flow.

In Table 8.1, we can see that all the restaurants show some form of consistency in their revenue from year to year, which is a good sign. As such, these four companies have passed the first performance indicator test.

As shown in Table 8.2, BreadTalk continues to show consistency in its net profit after tax. For ABR, net profit after tax decreased by 48 percent in 2006 to $4.04 million but regained its consistency from 2006 to 2010. After passing the first performance indicator, Sakae's and Tung Lok's net profits have proven to be highly inconsistent.

As shown in Table 8.3, BreadTalk's operational cash flow remains consistent. However, ABR's cash flow decreased by 38 percent in

Table 8.1   Revenue from Year 2005 to 2010 (S$ Millions)

Company	2005	2006	2007	2008	2009	2010
BreadTalk	95.2	123.5	156.6	212.2	246.4	302.8
ABR	123.3	135.3	154.4	184.4	188.4	230.4
Sakae	51.9	66.6	83.8	93.8	88.8	90.7
Tung Lok	82.8	64.9	69.8	75.9	73.4	81.3

Table 8.2   Net profit from Year 2005 to 2010 (S$ Millions)

Company	2005	2006	2007	2008	2009	2010
BreadTalk	1	4.3	7.3	7.77	11.1	11.26
ABR	10.3	4.04	3.83	8.35	9.08	11.04
Sakae	3.68	5.08	2.26	(3.75)	3.26	2.53
Tung Lok	(0.41)	1.38	1.05	0.37	(2.93)	0.65

Table 8.3   Operational cash flow from Year 2005 to 2010 (S$ Millions)

Company	2005	2006	2007	2008	2009	2010
BreadTalk	15	20	28.7	32.7	42.6	39.7
ABR	8.6	9.6	5.9	15.7	21.5	22.6
Sakae	6.3	7.6	8.2	1.8	3.8	7.2
Tung Lok	5.5	2.99	5.1	5.2	0.76	7.7

Table 8.4   Performance indicator of BreadTalk and ABR (5-year growth rate from 2005 to 2010)

Company	Revenue	Net Profit	Cash Flow
BreadTalk	26%	62.2%	21.4%
ABR	13.3%	1.4%	21.3%

2007—just as its net profit had decreased—but remained consistent from 2007 to 2010. Meanwhile, Sakae and Tung Lok were inconsistent in their figures for net operation cash flow.

At Stage 1, we would have eliminated Sakae and Tung Lok, due to their highly inconsistent net profits and operational cash flow. The final two companies that pass Stage 1 are BreadTalk and ABR, which will undergo further scrutiny in Stage 2.

Stage 2: Comparing the Compound Annual Growth Rate

In Stage 2, we shall compare the growth rate of every performance indicator of each company to see whether the company could become a multi-bagger. In this case, a growth rate of 15 percent and above is what we, as value-growth investors, are looking for. We shall use the compound annual growth rate (CAGR) formula, shown previously, to filter out potential growth companies based on real results.

From Table 8.4, the growth rate of BreadTalk, over the past six years, has increased more than 15 percent, compounded from 2005 to 2010. The lowest growth rate figure is for cash flow, which grew at 21.5 percent (more than 15 percent). Therefore, we will assume that BreadTalk is a growth company based on historical figures. For ABR, as its lowest compounded growth rate is 1.4 percent (less than 15 percent), we shall classify it as a slow grower (growing at less than 15 percent per annum). Thus, we will eliminate ABR in the screening process. That being said, you can continue to monitor ABR, if you feel that it has potential to grow even faster, after analyzing further information relating to its qualitative side. Until that is found to be true, we will eliminate ABR in Stage 2.

Stage 3: Finding Consistency or Increases In Margins

In Stage 3, we want to look at consistency in margin to spot a company's competitive advantage. Ideally, gross and net profit margin should be more than 20 and 10 percent, respectively. If a company's net profit margin is low, you have to ensure that the company has scalability power or is a low-cost producer. The gross profit for BreadTalk is shown in Table 8.5.

In Table 8.5, BreadTalk exhibits consistency in maintaining a high gross profit margin. This shows that BreadTalk is able to produce low-cost goods and sell them to consumers at a premium price. This is one of its competitive advantages. Now let us refer to BreadTalk's net profit margin in Table 8.6.

Based on net profit margins from 2005 to 2010, you can tell that BreadTalk has higher selling, general, and administrative expenses, resulting in lower net profits. However, BreadTalk possesses scalability power, as they have stores all over Singapore and overseas, including China. On one trip to Indonesia to do some scuttle-butting, we noticed, to our surprise, that there was a BreadTalk outlet in every shopping mall in the country (and there are many of them). Evidently, BreadTalk's core business in bread seems to suit the local palate as, at all times, the outlets appeared to be well patronized. Based on our observation, BreadTalk is believed to possess scalability power if it further expands its

Table 8.5 BreadTalk's gross profit margin (%) from Year 2005 to 2010

Company	2005	2006	2007	2008	2009	2010
BreadTalk	55	55	55.3	54.3	54.4	54.5

Table 8.6 BreadTalk's net profit margin (%) from Year 2005 to 2010

Company	2005	2006	2007	2008	2009	2010
BreadTalk	1.8	4.2	5.3	3.9	4.7	3.3

business. Moreover, BreadTalk has one of the highest revenues among the four companies.

Stage 4: Digging Further into a Company's Debt and Cash Position

At this stage, we shall look into a company's debt and cash position. As mentioned earlier, we do not want growth companies that are mainly financed by debts. They are likely to encounter problems and have trouble paying their debts if a crisis hits the company. In addition, it could create cash flow problems for the company and shareholders. However, having some debt (up to 50 percent of equity as the maximum limit) is not an issue if the growth company has a substantial amount of cash flow to meet principal and interest repayments without stressing its balance sheet; the reason being that it can enhance shareholders' returns. However, this should not be done to the extent that the company becomes overleveraged.

With cash amounting to S$71.1 million in 2010, BreadTalk has no problem covering its short- and long-term debts. Moreover, its debt to equity ratio was only at 0.28. In which case, a good and safe

Debt to equity ratio does not show how well a company can grow, but how much the company is gearing for every dollar of its net worth.

growth company must have its debt to equity ratio lower than 0.5. Remember, debt to equity ratio does not show how well a company can grow, but how much the company is gearing for every dollar of its net worth. Based on the given information in Table 8.7, this company possesses a good debt control structure.

Stage 5: Digging Further into Other Numbers to Confirm Your Pick

After the screening process in the first four stages, Stage 5 serves to confirm your decision when a company's numbers are studied in greater depth. We start off with the company's return on equity (ROE).

Table 8.7 BreadTalk's debt and cash position in 2010

Company	Cash (S$ Millions)	Total Debt (S$ Millions)	Equity (S$ Millions)	Debt to Equity Ratio (x)
BreadTalk	71.1	19.3	68.56	0.28

As shown in Table 8.8, BreadTalk was able to maintain an ROE of 14.5 to 18.2 percent between 2006 and 2010. Based on this piece of information, we can say that BreadTalk's management team has been utilizing its shareholders' money well.

From 2005 to 2010, BreadTalk displayed a high capital expenditure (CAPEX) ratio percentage (see Table 8.9). Here, BreadTalk's high CAPEX ratio is due to its widespread expansion plans in Singapore and overseas markets. Moreover, it is also justified with increasing revenue and profits. When determining a growth company, it is important to constantly check its CAPEX ratio against its revenue and profit figures. Higher CAPEX must be justified with higher revenue and earnings. Otherwise, it can be assumed that money spent (more than net profit) for development has not been well spent.

In this case, BreadTalk's operating cash flow, as seen in Table 8.10, is still higher than its CAPEX ratio, which still gives the business a positive free cash flow. This is deemed to be a good sign, as it suggests that their expansion is bringing cash in. To have a better understanding of CAPEX ratio, we will have to assess the next important figure: free cash flow.

In Table 8.10, BreadTalk's free cash-flow amount has not been very consistent. To generate higher revenue and profits, BreadTalk constantly needs to invest a huge amount of capital back into its business. Although BreadTalk had a CAPEX ratio of

Table 8.8   BreadTalk's return on equity (%) from Year 2005 to 2010

Company	2005	2006	2007	2008	2009	2010
BreadTalk	5	15.6	16.5	14.7	18.2	14.5

Table 8.9   BreadTalk's CAPEX ratio (%) from Year 2005 to 2010

Company	2005	2006	2007	2008	2009	2010
BreadTalk	802%	350%	212%	306%	207%	365%

Table 8.10   BreadTalk's free cash flow from Year 2005 to 2010 (S$ Million)

Company	2005	2006	2007	2008	2009	2010
BreadTalk	0.98	2	10.7	7.4	18.5	8.96

Table 8.11 BreadTalk's dividend payout ratio (%) from Year 2005 to 2010

Company	2005	2006	2007	2008	2009	2010
BreadTalk	0%	0%	25%	27%	31%	23.4%

more than 300 percent in 2010, it still generated a positive cash flow of $8.96 million.

In 2007, BreadTalk started to pay dividends. From then on, the dividend payout ratio consistently exceeded 20 percent, as shown in Table 8.11. Moving forward, this ratio is likely to stay from 20 to 30 percent as the expansion plan takes shape. Not to forget that BreadTalk is a growth company, and we prefer a growth company to finance its expansion using internal cash, rather than through the issuing of additional shares.

Conclusion

Based on our analysis, we conclude that BreadTalk has passed the five stages of screening.

Stage 1: BreadTalk and ABR display consistency in key performance indicators.

Stage 2: BreadTalk is a growth company and ABR is not.

Stage 3: BreadTalk has scalability power even though it has low net profit margins.

Stage 4: BreadTalk has conservative debt and a large amount of cash in its balance sheet that can help the business meet its short-term and long-term debt obligations.

Stage 5: BreadTalk has a high CAPEX ratio but is still able to generate positive free cash flow to shareholders. In addition, it has a consistent ROE ratio, free cash flow, and dividend payout ratio.

We can thus conclude that BreadTalk is a good growth company. Having said that, this screening method (using numbers alone) is useful only in uncovering good growth companies. By depending on

It would be extremely dangerous (e.g., value traps) if you rely solely on numbers and valuation alone when purchasing a particular stock.

numbers alone, value-growth investors are only made aware of one-quarter of the overall story. Value-growth investors should also look at a company's qualitative considerations, such as its business and management.

In this case, homework needs to be done to study BreadTalk further before acquiring its shares. It would be extremely dangerous (e.g., value traps) if you rely solely on numbers and valuation alone when purchasing a particular stock. With this, we will teach you how you can implement the Jigsaw Puzzle Model to support your decisions in buying, monitoring, or selling any stocks.

Buy, Monitor, and Sell

After a company passes a series of screenings, when exactly should you buy this company's stock? When it comes to buying, monitoring, and selling of stocks, when is the best time to buy and sell?

By now, you should know that not all growth companies have the potential to grow further, perhaps owing to a lack of competent management. Therefore, it is very important to do your homework, by assessing all four pieces of the Jigsaw Puzzle Model, before you even buy a single stock. A value-growth investor must go the extra mile by doing additional work, such as scuttle-butting, to find a good growth company that can generate superior returns in the long run.

It may sound easy, that simply by mastering each of the four chapters on business, management, numbers, and valuation, you would be able to ascertain a growth company. However, its execution is more difficult than it seems, as you must know how to use this model wisely and effectively. So, even if you are familiar with a company's products and services, its business model, and its competitive advantages, if any, there are still other considerations that need to come into play. Even if there appears to be good reason to buy a stock, it is still time for you to own its stock yet.

For instance, in 2010, Gardenia remained one of the top brands in Singapore, despite increasing competition. This brand is owned by QAF Ltd; one of its business segments comprises food manufacturing, bakery, and primary production. In addition, the company has also successfully developed its own in-house brand, Cow Head (milk and dairy products), which is widely distributed in Singapore and Southeast Asian countries. In Australia, QAF holds about 20 percent market share as a meat producer, compared to its main

Table 8.12   Inconsistent business numbers from year to year

Company	QAF (S$ million)					
	2005	2006	2007	2008	2009	2010
Revenue	885.8	992	1076	840	855	856.4
Net Profit	11.4	19.5	14.1	−29	59.3	56.8
Operation Cash Flow	5.4	−12.8	−54.3	102.9	89.4	101.4

competitor, which holds about 7 percent of the market. While QAF can be classified as a company with a wide moat, it is still not a great investment in our opinion. Why? Simply because it does not fulfill one of the four components in the Jigsaw Puzzle Model: The financial numbers are inconsistent. Owing to this inconsistency, our projection of its intrinsic value becomes inaccurate.

Even though Gardenia might be a good brand with a strong moat, QAF is a company that will most definitely not appear on our list, as the numbers simply tell us a different story. As shown by the figures in Table 8.12, QAF's growth has been stagnant for the past six years. In fact, it has found itself in a position and size that makes it quite difficult to expand further. Therefore, it is not considered a growth company.

Buy, Buy, and Buy

The best time to buy is when everyone is selling. Yes, you heard right—buy when everyone is selling! Such selling normally happens during a recession or when there is bad news about a company. Sure, it is a scary proposition to buy when everyone else is selling. But there are reasons for doing so.

Before you buy a stake in a company, find out why everyone is selling frantically. There is always a reason why a growth company is cheap. When someone is selling a stock to you, they must know something that you do not. Thus, it is your duty to find out what these reasons are. It could be an emotional reaction when investors look at falling prices in the market. It could be that the company reported disappointing results. Get your facts right, and make sure the problems are temporary. As always, it is best to use the Jigsaw Puzzle Model to assist you in your decision to buy.

The best time to buy is when everyone is selling.

We will buy only when the growth company has fulfilled all the four pieces of the Jigsaw Puzzle Model as follows:

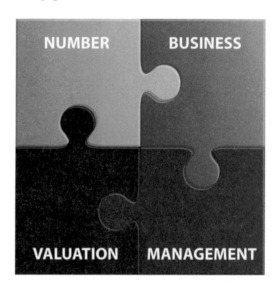

Business—It should have a simple business model with strong moats protecting it from competitors. These moats can be in the form of brands, being the lowest-cost producer, high switching cost, economies of scale, or recurring revenue in nature. Understand their risks thoroughly! You could take advantage of those who are selling their stocks to you because they either panicked or do not understand their risks well. In which case, we need to ascertain that a company's expansion plan is working out well.

Management—At the same time, the company should be managed by people whom you trust and feel that it is safe for them to manage your money. Such a management team needs to be aligned with shareholders' interests. When insiders (e.g., CEO, CFO, or other substantial shareholders) buy back shares, they are putting their own money in and increasing their percentage of ownership. These are people who know something that others do not know; they buy because they believe the company is undervalued, which demonstrates their confidence in the outlook of the company. Since no one knows a company better than insiders, such a sign is positive. This is especially true if more than one insider is buying extensively during the same period. It has to be said that there are times where management uses the company's cash to buy more of its stocks as well. We also look for management that has a substantial stake in the company.

Numbers—The company must be fundamentally healthy. In other words, all the numbers in the financial statements must fall within the required threshold. Here, our projections will be more accurate when a company has a great business and competent management with consistent past earnings.

Valuation—This lets us know at what price we should consider paying when buying a stock, or vice versa. If, at this point of analysis, after calculating the price-to-earnings-to-growth (PEG) ratio and intrinsic value, we find that Mr. Market is selling at a great discount with a high margin of safety, say more than 50 percent, we will take action and buy this company.

In summary, you buy only when you fully understand the business. For that, you need to understand how the company earns profits through its day-to-day operations or from different divisions. The business should be simple and easy to understand or within your circle of competence. You know what is protecting the company from outside competitors and who the competitors are. You understand the risks well. You are confident that there is room for expansion or potential growth in the company's business. The management is found to be trustworthy, candid in reporting, aligned to shareholders' interests, and possesses a strong track record. They should constantly seek new ways to increase shareholders' value, either through expansion of its current business or by acquiring new businesses.

Growth companies should show consistent performances in revenue, earnings, and operations cash flow. The company yields good gross profits and net profit margins that are higher than its competitors. It should have a high ROE of more than 15 percent and low gearing ratio (low gearing is equal to low debt to equity ratio) of less than 0.5. As there are profits, cash amounts would increase if the management is able to keep the CAPEX ratio less than 80 percent or generate positive free cash flow. Last, we should have a margin of safety of a minimum of 50 percent in order to maximize our return and lower our risks in the long run. In other words, buy growth companies when they are undervalued. It is even better if the PEG ratio is less than 0.5, because you pay not more than half of its growth rate. If every one of these metrics has been fulfilled, this company is very likely to be a successful growth company. Value-growth investors must take action after they have substantiated all their findings or when all four pieces of the Jigsaw Puzzle Model come together seamlessly.

In June 2010, we applied the Jigsaw Puzzle Model to Design Studio, and it worked very well. The company was growing at a rate of more than 30 percent in the past four years (2005 to 2009), be it based on revenue, net profits, or operations cash flow. It has a great business with a strong work order book in hand and is run by a management team that has an excellent track record, is trustworthy, and is aligned to shareholders' interests. At the same time, the numbers were good, with net profit margin and returns on equity at 18 percent and 29 percent, respectively, in 2009. It displayed a consistent drop in ratio of debt to equity from more than 1 in 2005 to its new low of nearly zero in 2009. Last but not least, the company has been consistently generating free cash flow to share-holders with a low CAPEX ratio of less than 50 percent in the past four consecutive years. At that time, we bought its shares at S$0.45, when its intrinsic value was at more than S$0.80. With additional net cash, it gave us a margin of safety of more than 50 percent. Moreover, the PEG ratio was less than 0.4! In this case, Design Studio has fulfilled all four pieces of the Jigsaw Puzzle Model, and proved to be a good opportunity for us to invest in a growth com-pany at a bargain price.

That being said, you might still suffer losses if you had bought at the right price but into the wrong business or management. Meanwhile, buying the right business or management with the wrong fundamentals (numbers) and price (valuation) could result in underperformance compared to the rest of the market. The key is to use the model to guide you and make sure all the pieces are fulfilled before you purchase a stock.

Monitor, Monitor, and Monitor

Monitoring is important in investing. It is a combination that involves both the art and science of evaluating a compa-ny's past performance, its latest news, as well as management activities. The main reason why we monitor a company is to know whether the company that we have invested in (or have not) is doing well, or if there is an opportunity to purchase or increase our stake in the company. Or, in relation to the Jigsaw Puzzle Model, that we have not misplaced a piece of the puzzle after we bought a growth company.

When we first discovered Design Studio, it was trading at S$0.65. This gave us a low margin of safety (less than 50 percent) with the intrinsic value estimated at S$0.80, based on zero percent growth. In this case, we adopted a wait-and-see approach as we continued to monitor the stocks. We wanted to see if Mr. Market would offer us a good price to buy. Lo and behold, the company announced that it was involved in a lawsuit. Its share price dropped from S$0.65 to S$0.45!

We were blessed to have bought the stocks at a bargain price. Indeed, patience is a virtue! As historical data has shown, what goes up must come down. The moral of the story is to have a wish list under your portfolio and cash to invest when the time ripens. As it is, a potential growth company is not being offered at a bargain price every time. When the market is booming, the stocks would be overvalued. In this case, these companies might have fulfilled three pieces (business, management, and numbers) of the Jigsaw Puzzle but are still not good stocks to buy, as their value is overpriced. This is often the case when the market is good.

During such times, it is strongly recommended that you continue to monitor these stocks, as there will be a time when Mr. Market will come back to you with a new, lower offer price. A good example of this was our encounter with Q&M Dental Group. In this case, we like the company's business model and management. However, it has yet to prove itself with numbers, due to its relatively short track record (listed for only a year at that point of analysis). The stock was also overpriced (even at 15 percent growth rate) based on our estimation. Applying the model, Q&M Dental has met two pieces—business and management. While the pieces on numbers and valuation are yet to be fulfilled, we would wait patiently for the company to go on sale one day. In this case, we would continue to monitor the business for an additional two years to better judge its financial performance. With a sufficient margin of safety, it would protect our downside risks in case the expansion plans in local and overseas markets do not work out as smoothly as planned. In our opinion, there is no harm in being patient and monitoring the situation.

Upon discovering a potential fast grower and acquiring a stake in it, your job as a value-growth investor has not yet come to an end. Thereafter, you must continue to monitor the shares, based

Have a wish list under your portfolio and have cash to invest when the time ripens.

on the four components of the Jigsaw Puzzle Model, every quarter. The main purpose is to be updated on the status of the company to ensure that everything is still in place and to look out for any irregularities that could lead to deteriorating fundamentals. In doing so, you want to ensure your initial deduction is still valid.

For instance, after we bought stocks of Design Studio at an undervalued price of $0.45, we continued to look out for any news or announcements made by the company (e.g., news or quarterly reports). We were also on the lookout for potential risks and were eager to attend its annual general meeting (AGM). We know that a growth company like Design Studio, which is growing at more than 15 percent per annum, would not grow forever. There would be a point at which growth will stagnate or even drop. For this reason, we owe it to ourselves to monitor the company.

While doing so, which could be over a course of a few months or even years, there would be times when you could have reaped a significant profit. But a successful value-growth investor must be patient. For average investors, on the other hand, being patient is not necessarily seen as a virtue, as they do not understand the power of compounding interest. In their opinion, sitting on cash is deemed useless as it depreciates over time. To the value-growth investor, however, it is all right to sit on cash when you simply cannot find any bargain stocks. In fact, you are actually better off keeping the cash when you are unable to find growth companies at a bargain price.

There would be a point at which growth will stagnate or even drop. For this reason, we owe it to ourselves to monitor the company.

Moreover, with cash on hand, you do not need to sell existing stocks at a cheap price (before they reach their intrinsic value) when you want to invest in a more attractive stock. When the opportunity arises for you to invest in undervalued stocks with a margin of safety at more than

50 percent, you need not sell existing stocks that have been bought when it was undervalued—stocks that require time for them to realize their intrinsic value. Without touching your existing portfolio, you could invest in another gem with the cash you are sitting on. As a result, the potential return of additional undervalued stock in your portfolio would be even greater. In the long run, you are more likely to earn larger profits. For this reason, you should just sit on cash if you are unable to find any bargain growth companies. Instead, you should wait until you find one! Here, the monitoring process can be carried out offline and/or online. There are two ways by which you can monitor them.

Online Monitoring

Shareinvestors.com—This is a paid subscription-based platform that is run and managed by Singapore Press Holding (SPH). This website has a function called portfolio. It has been modified in such a way that investors can get all the necessary information they need, including news, insider trading, and dividend amounts, as well as information on upcoming AGMs. On this website, the fundamental data includes a company's financial statements, such as income statement, balance sheet, and cash-flow statement. On top of that, most of the financial ratios, like ROE, debt to equity, and net profit margin, as well as basic valuation ratios such as price-to-equity (PE) ratio and P/B ratio, have already been calculated for investors, which saves us a lot of time.

In addition, there are other good tools, such as stock watch list. Most worthy of mention is the stock filter tool, which has made our life so much easier since we started to use this platform. With these tools, we can screen for potential growth companies quickly and purchase them at an undervalued price within a short time frame.

Other Financial Websites—Websites like MSN Money Central, Yahoo Finance, and Investing Week also provide good analytical tools for you to customize your investment portfolio. One of our favorite monitoring tools is a ShareInvestor account. With so much information housed in one account, it is saves a great deal of time.

Brokerage Account—A good way to monitor stocks is through your own stock broker account. It often provides in-depth analysis about some companies. It provides the market value of companies each working day. In addition, it also allows you to know whether your investment has gained or lost value based on the percentage of your initial buying price. However, investors should exercise independent thinking. In other words, the information provided by analysts should only be taken as a source of reference and not be used for decision making. An example of a brokerage firm in Asia is CIMB.

Company Website—Get yourself on the mailing list for any press releases a company sends. To do so, approach an investor relations officer to keep you informed of the company's latest happenings. In our opinion, this method of obtaining a company's information is extremely useful when you do not have a ShareInvestor account.

Every quarter, a company will announce its unaudited financial statement to retail investors. Investors must be kept informed about these statements. With the release of new financial statements, new financial ratios and intrinsic value should also be worked out. As value-growth investors, we would tend to place more emphasis on annual, rather than quarterly, results, as we are focused on a company's long-term financial standing. Nonetheless, when we do monitor a company's quarterly results, we need to remember that some companies are subjected to seasonal sales. For instance, Soup Restaurant is likely to see sales surge during the Chinese New Year season.

We recount our recent experiences—a road construction business, which our fund vested in, lost numerous contracts consecutively during the tendering process, and the bottom line shown on their quarterly statement has not been encouraging. The nature of business is not as predictable when compared to a healthcare business. As such, the company needs to constantly bid for new projects. Thus, revenues and earnings are foggy in the mid- to long term. At least, the only feasibility we could see is their large chunk of order books which could sustain them for a couple of years. A decision was needed during the discussion. But, happily, no action was taken.

Offline Process

Investors should keep themselves updated about a company's happenings through media sources such as newspapers and magazines (e.g. CEO's interview). However, do not let the media influence your decision when it comes to investing. Instead, it should simply serve as a source of information. You should avoid hot stocks and tips obtained from the media.

Scuttle-butting—Before you buy the stocks of a company, you have to perform scuttle-butting on both its management and business operations. When it comes to scuttle-butting a company's business operations, it is a good idea to do so by directly going to the business's operation site to check on the number of customers, talk to the suppliers or anyone in that particular industry. This may be carried out quarterly or annually.

For instance, after buying into Japan Food, we continued to perform scuttle-butting by visiting some of its restaurants during peak and nonpeak periods to ensure that the company's business is operating well. Here scuttle-butting is carried out in spite of our confidence in the business to flourish over the course of the next ten years. Through scuttle-butting, we can ascertain that the company still has growth present. And, if we found otherwise, we would at least spot the first few signs of trouble before analysts or fund managers are made aware of them.

In relation to the management of a company, it is important for you to attend the company's AGM before you place a high stake in the company, such as purchasing a lot of shares in a company that you believe is a potential growth company. With this, you are allowed to attend the company's AGM or extraordinary general meeting when necessary. Even though the cost of doing so is high, it allows you to be better informed about your investment and, as a result, take better measures against suffering from huge investment losses when things do not turn out well. During such meetings, you could pose questions that directly allay your concerns. By having such a stake in a company, you will also be better informed by the management about the company's performance via an annual report delivered to your doorstep.

Sell, Sell, and Sell

If the company continues to fulfill your predetermined criteria to buy, you may hold it for as long as you want to, as you are on course to greater riches. In doing so, you can allow it to compound longer. In relation to how long you should hold onto stocks, it must be said that Warren Buffett's holding period is forever. As value-growth investors, we do not sell even when the price has gone up. Instead of merely looking at price as an indicator, components in the Jigsaw Puzzle Model offer insight as to when you can sell stocks of a growth company. For instance, if one of the pieces of the puzzle starts to deteriorate, say, numbers have slipped, and it no longer meets the criteria to hold, it is probably time to sell your stocks. After all, this causes the Jigsaw Puzzle to be incomplete, thereby going against our initial reason for wanting to hold a specific stock.

Warren Buffett's holding period is forever.

Business—We sell our shares in a company when the core business of the company starts to veer into a new industry that it is not capable of being successful in. We also sell our shares in a company when a failed product surfaces or when stiff competition sets in, such that the company can no longer maintain its moat.

There will surely come a point when the growth rate of a growth company will either slow down or stagnate. When the growth rate of a company starts to slow down during expansion (i.e., opening new stores in local or overseas markets), it is a telltale sign that its growth has reached its limit. Even though many companies like to blame poor economic conditions for stagnation or a drop in sales, we find that this is often not the main contributing factor to a slower growth. In fact, a promising growth company should still be able to continue opening new stores in new markets to target new consumers. For this reason, it is very important to keep monitoring a growth company and be kept aware of its sales figure.

Management—We sell our stakes in a company when its main shareholders or internal management starts to significantly divest their shares. However, selling of shares by main shareholders need not necessarily suggest that something is amiss. Sometimes the shareholder in question might need the money for personal reasons. However, you must take note if more insiders are selling away a large chunk of shares within a short period of time; it might mean that there is trouble ahead for the company or that management feels that the company is being overvalued. We should also sell our shares when key management members, especially the founders, are involved in a serious fraud case. However, if a problem is deemed to be temporary and does not affect the nature of the business (e.g., many people are still using their services or products), we should buy more of a company's shares when the market is still punishing it. In this case, the key is in determining whether the company is facing a short-term or long-term problem. Frequent changes in key management, such as CEO, CFO, COO, or auditor is an indicator that something is wrong with the management.

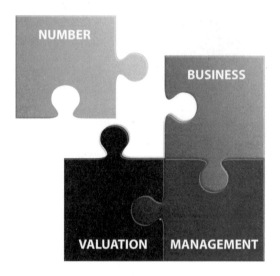

Numbers—We sell our stakes in a company when its fundamentals start to experience significant shifts. Holding onto a stock that no longer has strong fundamentals would hurt us in the long run. One such example is when a company with zero or low debt starts to increase its borrowing from the bank way above its equity (debt to equity ratio >1), or it has reported sharp decline in earnings in several consecutive quarters. Since we abide by the theory that stocks with good fundamentals will eventually reward us in the long run, there is no reason to hold onto a stock once its numbers become less promising.

Valuation—We sell shares of a company when its price hits its intrinsic value, is overvalued with a negative margin of safety, or the PEG ratio is more than 1. Although we do not recommend selling a stock while every other piece of the puzzle is still intact, you should sell your stocks when it they no longer meet the valuation criteria. One such example is when a company's historical PE ratio starts to increase and overshoots the mark by 20 times. In which case, the PE ratio is equal or twice its growth rate, resulting in a PEG ratio of more than 1.5 and a price that is way above its intrinsic value. When any two criteria shift the valuation piece out of the Jigsaw Puzzle Model, an investor should consider selling the stock for a profit. That being said, you still have to re examine your initial reason for buying this stock, for it is possible for the company to move on and pick up on its share price over time. If you believe that the value of the company will increase, you can continue to hold onto it and work out its new intrinsic value. If you believe that the company is incapable of growing at the same rate, you can sell it off and find a new bargain growth stock to invest in.

Table 8.13 Comparison between Company A and Company B for a possible switch

	PE Ratio	EPS Growth (%)	PEG Ratio	If PEG raise to 1 (%)
Company A	15	20	0.75	33%
Company B	7	20	0.35	185%

The Jigsaw Puzzle Model aside, if everyone in the stock market is talking about the stock—every magazine is featuring it and is highly recommended by analysts—it is time to sell. It is also time to sell when institutional investors start to own more than 20 percent of the stock.

Sometimes, another consideration to sell is when there are better companies out there that are more attractive than the companies you currently own. This could be because you managed to find a better bargain—a good business run by a great management and backed with stronger figures. However, good investments that are offered at a bargain price are hard to find during good times. But if you spot one, you can consider a switch. Let us look at a possible switch in the following example in Table 8.13.

In this case, let us assume that both companies' business, management, and numbers have been fulfilled. Using the information found in Table 8.13, you will find that Company B is a better bargain. Given the same growth rate, Company B is trading at 7 times its earnings, while Company A is trading at 15 times it earnings. Between the two, Company B has a PEG ratio that is far more attractive than that of Company A. Furthermore, the return for Company B increased by 185 percent, while the return for Company A only increased by 33 percent. Based on these figures, you are better off selling your shares in Company A and reinvesting in Company B for higher profits.

If everyone in the stock market is talking about the stock—every magazine is featuring it and is highly recommended by analysts—it is time to sell.

Most important, value-growth investors must ignore all noises relating to economic outlook, be it boom or doom. This is especially true when such forecasts are made by analysts, as they are paid to do so and draw a commission. As a value-growth investor, your decision to buy or sell a stock is not dependent on market buzz but dependent on the Jigsaw Puzzle Model, where you make your decisions based on your findings and analysis.

Summary

- Screening (Using Numbers against Competitors)
  Stage 1: Increasing trends of revenue, net profit, and cash flow
  Stage 2: Compare growth rates (CAGR > 15 percent)
  Stage 3: Consistent margins
  Stage 4: Debt to equity ratio < 0.5 and prefer Cash > Debt
  Stage 5: Consistent ROE (>15 percent), CAPEX (<80 percent).
     Otherwise, there must be positive free cash flow and a dividend payout ratio of <50 percent
- Buying Process (Jigsaw Puzzle Model)
  All these pieces must be fulfilled:
  Business—PASS
  Management—PASS
  Number—PASS
  Valuation—PASS
- Monitoring Process
  Monitor once per quarter or year, using the Jigsaw Puzzle Model after you have (or have not) purchased a stock.
  Sit on CASH and wait for an opportunity if you are unable to find any bargain stocks.
  Proceed to sell when any of the puzzle pieces start to fall apart.
- Selling Process (Jigsaw Puzzle Model)
  If one of the following fails, it fulfills the selling criteria:
  Business—FAIL
  Management—FAIL
  Number—FAIL
  Valuation—FAIL

CHAPTER 9

Portfolio Management for Growth Companies

Understanding Your Portfolio

This chapter is about the allocation of capital for growth companies in your existing portfolio. Before we discuss how you can allocate your money to growth companies, we want to let you know that, although we attempt to generate a consistent return of more than 15 percent over a long period of time, you might not see such consistent returns year after year. In fact, your return might even be negative in some years.

For instance, if you bought a stock at $1, you might have realized a gain of 30 percent if the stock price had shot up to $1.30 a month later. Thereafter, the price might have dipped from $1.30 to $0.90, resulting in a return of −10 percent. Due to fluctuations in market prices, the return on your portfolio understandably varies. In the short term, market volatility is unpredictable. However, in the long run, the market should be more efficient, and you should be able to reap this return if you purchased a growth company at an undervalued price.

One of the most frequently asked questions when it comes to allocating capital to growth companies is "Should I place all my eggs into one basket and watch over it, or should I place my eggs in several different baskets to lower my risks?" Again, this is not a one-size-fits-all portfolio management strategy. The allocation has to be dependent on your risk appetite and age profile. Let's go through them in more details.

Types of Diversification

The main objective of diversification is to protect your investment from factors such as unpredictable events that may impact a company or your own ignorance (missing certain risks involved). From the very beginning of this book, we have outlined ways to reduce possible investment risks and explore potential future growth drivers among growth companies. We have also taught you how to gather the right facts and information from the right sources.

So, with all these measures and considerations, would it still be dangerous for you to place all your savings in a single company? Yes. Although you have taken care to choose companies that have a low debt, a high return on equity (ROE), with a management that you trust, among other considerations, some of these companies are be rather small and can be highly unstable during their initial stage of expansion. As it is, every company presents some inherent risks. No matter how well your analysis is carried out, companies could still be plagued by unexpected events (e.g., fraud, natural disaster). For instance, during the SARS period, the majority of companies in Singapore were badly affected.

The main objective of diversification is to protect your investment from factors such as unpredictable events that may impact a company or your own ignorance (missing certain risks involved).

If anything, risks are unavoidable when it comes to investing. In view of such potential risks, because you do not know what you do not know, it is best to diversify your capital across multiple stocks or different industries to reduce being exposed to greater risk. We have classified three types of diversification: personal, company, and industry. Here, *personal diversification* is with regard to your personal portfolio, where you might possess unit trusts, exchange traded funds (ETF), or properties, and so on. *Company diversification* is the strategic diversification planned by the management to spread the risk across its internal business. Finally, *industry diversification* suggests that you hold different growth companies in different industries.

Personal Diversification

Everybody has a different appetite for risk. Investors who are under 25 years of age, very much like us, are risk takers, as compared to older investors. Naturally, we possess more time and energy to invest in growth companies. Although growth companies are our target, we know better than to place all our eggs into one basket. In other words, we do not channel all our cash into a single growth company. Instead, we prefer to distribute our risks evenly, by diversifying into various companies in different industries. In contrast, older investors may choose to invest in more stable and recession-proof companies, so that they are paid dividends even during recessionary times. This group of investors is more willing to invest more money into mature companies, in the hopes of receiving a higher dividend to fund their retirement.

Most Singaporeans are, in fact, quite well diversified. For starters, we contribute 20 percent of our incomes to the Central Provident Fund board (CPF), where we indirectly set aside 20 percent of our earnings for our retirement. Apart from using this amount to fund our future retirement, some people may use it to buy a house. In doing so, housing then becomes an asset in which most Singaporeans place their money. In this case, housing then becomes a long-term investment in which short-term price fluctuations would not affect owners who treat this asset as their principal residence. Eventually, they would make money in the long run just by holding onto their property. Hence, investing in your own home is always a good strategy.

Housing aside, growth companies are a good form of investment if you are young. With a longer window of time to invest, you can hold onto its shares and earn profits in the long run. This is in comparison with an older investor who needs to access these funds within a shorter time frame to fund his or her retirement needs. Having said that, you should limit your total stock holding to fewer than 10 companies in a developed country like Singapore, regardless of your age and investment appetite. This makes its more manageable for you to monitor and stay informed about the companies' activities.

If you are overdiversified, say, with 50 companies in your investment portfolio, you might end up with a return that is equivalent to the market's average—the Straits Times Index (STI) in this case, or worse. Conversely, if you place all your money into only one or two growth companies, you can easily end up losing a lot of money when these companies meet with a mishap. On the other hand, you could also make a lot of money if these two companies experience further growth in the long run. In any case, capital preservation is more important in the world of investing. For this reason, we have to first protect our downside. As Warren Buffett pointed out, the number one rule in investing is *never lose money*. And diversification is one way to lower our risks of losing capital.

> The number one rule in investing is never lose money.
> —*Warren Buffett*

Some investors might recommend that you diversify your portfolio in overseas markets. But, before you invest in companies abroad, you should always familiarize yourself with the country and its financial regulations, not just the companies. For example, some investors might feel uncomfortable with the management or political instability in Indonesia, or are put off by a high corruption rate in the country. Meanwhile, companies listed in China or Hong Kong might be subject to lots of corporate governance issues, on top of having unreliable management that could simply siphon a company's funds and flee. In view of these potential risks, your portfolio should have more than 10, but fewer than 20, companies, should you choose to invest in developing countries.

Company Diversification

Say you are working in a company that is listed on the Singapore Exchange (SGX) and you buy your own company shares. In other words, you are placing your job and investment in one single basket. In this case, should anything happen to the company, you would not only lose your job but also your investment.

For example, when ENRON, an American energy company, went bankrupt as a result of irregular accounting and poor financial reporting, employees lost their jobs and money invested in the company's pension fund when the scandal broke out. However, there is nothing wrong with investing your own savings into your company, if you are truly confident that the company will grow and prosper over the long haul. In this case, you may stand to benefit from insider information and have an edge over outside investors. Moreover, you are even able to perform scuttle-butting across different departments within the company. On top of that, you can rightfully access exclusive information about the company and gain a more in-depth insight into the management's capabilities and plans.

In relation to this, some companies are well diversified into various industries. Some of these companies have several core businesses that spread across different industries or countries. For instance, owning Boustead is almost like owning four different classes of stock, ranging from geospatial, real estate, wastewater management, and engineering solutions. Companies such as WingTaiAsia are also well diversified across retail and property industries. Meanwhile, Fraser & Neave is well diversified in areas like beverages and real estate.

There are also many companies that are diversified internationally as well. A company like Design Studio has diversified its business to Dubai and all across Asia. These companies are said to be well diversified across different countries, and thus provide a cushion for investors, should a country temporarily plunge into crisis. In addition, growth companies can sometimes be well diversified across many industries, where the competency of their management lies in the respective industry that they manage. In such instances, these companies provide a larger playing field where investors would be exposed to lower risks.

Industry Diversification

As of June 2011, the SGX had more than 700 companies from different industries listed on the main board. With so many companies to choose from, you can pick the best growth companies of each industry to effectively distribute your risks. For instance, the food and beverage (F&B) industry is more resistant during a downturn compared to the construction industry. So, within the F&B industry, you could pick up a company like Japan Food, analyze it, and decide if it is a better option than its competitors. If you have a great edge in the engineering industry (e.g., within your circle of competence), you could find a growth company in that industry as well.

The bottom line is that the more you understand a certain stock, the more investment weight you should give it in your portfolio. With the bulk of your portfolio being directed to growth companies, the remaining percentage can be allocated to blue-chip companies, as such companies are monopolies that command a competitive advantage. Even though these are not growth companies, they hand out handsome dividends each year. However, these blue-chip companies yield lower returns from capital appreciation and dividend growth, as compared to smaller and younger growth companies.

With respect to industry diversification, owning shares in three F&B companies is not exactly a wise strategy.

When choosing a growth company, it must be emphasized that they need not originate from a hot or growing industry. Rather, these must be companies that offer much room for expansion, as ascertained using scuttle-butting or figures obtained from the company's annual reports. With respect to industry diversification, owning shares in three F&B companies is not exactly a wise strategy, as they belong to the same industry.

The Sky Is the Limit

Unlike trading with leverage, where you can potentially make a lot of money or go bankrupt all in a second's notice, value-growth investing lives up to being one of the most effectual investment styles we have found, as it enables you to similarly win big, but without the risk of going bankrupt. In this light, value-growth investing is a more forgiving investment approach, as you do not have to be 100 percent correct in every stock that you pick. Ultimately, our intention is for you to invest in growth companies that have a higher probability of being right than wrong. As long as the number of times that you are right outweighs the times that you are wrong, you are more likely to find yourself earning quite a substantial profit, based on the compounding principle, in the long run.

It can be said that there is a limit to losing, but no limits to winning!

Even if a stock is found to be wrong, so to speak, your losses will be limited. For instance, in a portfolio of 10 growth companies, you just need to have a minimum of five right stocks to become a successful investor and get a high return. So, if you place $10,000 into 10 different growth companies, amounting to a total investment of

$100,000, the maximum you can lose is $50,000. In this case, you only need to have stakes in three successful growth companies to be a very successful investor. If it is indeed true, and that the three companies are 10-baggers, your return works out to be $300,000 or more. So, even with a loss of $50,000, you would still reap a $250,000 profit. With this understanding, it can be said that there is a limit to losing, but no limit to winning! As long as the Jigsaw Puzzle Model remains intact for a particular stock, you are well on your way to enjoying unlimited riches.

Summary

- Diversification Strategy in
    - Developed Countries: < 10 stocks
    - Developing Countries: 10 to 20 stocks
- Some companies are pretty well diversified internally, be it locally or internationally.
- Diversify the 10 stocks (developed countries) across different industries.
- Place a higher percentage of your total invested fund in a growth company in the industry that you understand most.

10

Avoid Common Mistakes

The Dos and Don'ts of Investing

To become a successful investor, we need to know why most investors fail. In doing so, we hope to learn from someone else's mistakes, so that we can be spared from making them. In fact, it must be said that most successful investors, such as Warren Buffett, John Neff, and Peter Lynch, are able to beat the market countless times, not because they are smarter, but because they have learned from mistakes they made along the way. So important is learning from failure that Charlie Munger, vice chairman and partner of Warren Buffett at Berkshire Hathaway, first studies how a business can fail before exploring ways that it can become successful. In other words, he would first learn about potential risks, so that he can understand and avoid them. Considering how this approach can add value to our investment strategies, this chapter will be dedicated to unraveling some of the common mistakes in investing.

Mistake 1: You Think You Are a Long-Term Investor but You Are Really a Speculator

You may think like a long-term investor but act like a speculator who deals in the stock market. In that, you make your investment decisions based on the rise and fall of prices. However, if you are truly convinced of the prospects of being a value-growth investor, you should use the tips presented in this book and curb your speculative ways. Speculation is a risky investment strategy in which you tend to move with the crowd (herding) rather than going against it.

Typically, short-term traders are guilty of investment decisions that are purely speculative, and made without any assessment. They define their success based on the outcome of their invest-ment, and not on the process of analyzing the factors that would affect the price of a stock (e.g., fundamentals). If the price of the stock goes up in the short term, their investment would be con-sidered successful. Such success is really pure luck. Truly successful investors should be able to project their portfolio over the long run, to allow the principle of compounded interest to work its magic. Merely looking at the prices of stocks, which may or may not go up in the short term, does not generate consistent returns, because short-term market fluctuations are affected by market sen-timents, not value.

Speculation is a risky investment strategy in which you tend to move with the crowd (herding).

If you are a short-term trader who would like to become a value-growth investor, refrain from looking at stock prices every day, so that you are not tempted to trade. Monitor stocks from time to time by checking for news related to the company. If you must look at the price of a stock, we recommend you do so once a week or even once a month. Remember that, in the short term, stock prices fluctuate, but, over the long haul, stocks prices reflect the true value of a company. As value-growth investors, being patient ensures our success, as we allow our money to be compounded over time. Since we are not constantly looking at stock prices, we may run into a problem whereby we do not know for how much the stock is being traded. But that, in our opinion, is not a loss.

According to Warren Buffett, "Price is what you pay; value is what you get." Unlike short-term traders, we do not weigh a com-pany solely based on its stock price. If Stock A is trading at $0.50, as compared to Stock B, which is trading at $10, many investors would assume that Stock A is a better bargain because of its price. That cannot be further from the truth! It gets worse if they assume that the price of Stock A can easily increase fourfold to $2, for example, compared to Stock B, which is deemed unlikely to trade at $40. During the 2008–2009 financial crisis, Jardine Cycle & Carriage, a leading automotive manufacturer and distributor, was trading below S$10 in the first quarter of 2009, but its share price shot up to nearly S$40 in late 2010. This goes to show that judging how big a bargain a company is, based on its price alone, is misleading and inaccurate. Instead, investors should be taking into consideration the amount of profit being generated and the number of outstanding shares available.

Essentially, you should not value a company based on its price, but on its fundamentals. To us, price is illusion in the short term. With this under-

Judging how much of a bargain a company is, based on its price alone, is misleading and inaccurate.

standing, we will still hold the same number of shares even when the market and prices are down (except when a company issues additional new shares by way of bonus or right issues). When the economy does pick up, share prices will eventually go back to their intrinsic value where all the four pieces of the Jigsaw Puzzle Model would be once again intact.

Mistake 2: Timing the Market

We do not time the market, be it trending up or down. While some investors might try to time the buying of a stock to when it is at its absolute bottom, we, as value-growth investors, do not. If timing the bottom of the market were possible, you would not be reading this book. Instead of timing the market, we work out the intrinsic value of a company based on facts, not gut instincts. After all, we are not Paul the Octopus, who became famous for correctly predicting the outcome of the last eight games (including the finals) in the World Cup 2010 in South Africa.

When it comes to investing, there will be times when we buy a stock that has been priced low, only to find that the price drops further. This is fine, so long as you have reassessed all the pieces of the puzzle and everything is still intact. Using dollar cost averaging, it would average out your initial cost of purchase. To put it in simpler terms, let us say that, after you purchased a stock at $1, the stock plunges to $0.80. You decide to purchase the same number of shares you first bought, so that the average share price of both purchases will be $0.90 [($1.00 + $0.80) ÷ 2]. These are short-term fluctuations that do not impact long-term investors. As long as we have a broad margin of safety, we are still very safe! In fact, when prices drop, we are presented with a better bargain and a higher margin of safety.

Moreover, if you try to time the market, it will be very easy for you to get it wrong. Reading economic news does not help either. At the end of the day, no one knows for sure when the market will be bearish or bullish. Collectively, the market behaves just like an individual stock. When the market does go up, it may go even higher. Or it might drop and stagnate for a very long period of time. Eventually, it may take years for the market to realize its true value. A commonly held misconception about investing is that successful investing is when the price of a share increases after we have purchased it. However, successful investing should be thought of as the ability to generate consistent returns in the long run.

Successful investing should be thought of as the ability to generate consistent returns in the long run.

When it comes to successful investing, Warren Buffett has generated compounded rates of return of 20 to 25 percent when he managed Berkshire Hathaway. When he managed Fidelity, Peter Lynch had a track record of generating compounded rates consistently at more than 30 percent over the span of 13 years. As you can see, success is measured in the long run.

Most investors mistakenly think they would be able to spot signs of an upswing to trigger them to buy their shares, only to find themselves with a missed hit. Investing during a crisis, or when everyone expresses pessimism over a certain stock, requires investors to be comfortable with the fact that the price could go even lower. Thus, the main objective is not to time the market but to use dollar cost averaging if the price of an investment drops. Conversely, selling a stock during a boom market when its price is overvalued does not mean that the stock price has hit its highest point. It could go higher after you sell it. That does not matter to us because the end result would still be a gain on investment, as long as we have a margin of safety before we buy and sell it at a fairly or grossly overvalued price. Such is the beauty of a value-growth investing strategy.

Mistake 3: Investing in High-Technology and IPO Companies

Get to know the company behind the stock as thoroughly as possible. Remember, when you want to buy a stock, you are buying a stake in a company—you are becoming an owner. Approach a stock the same manner as you would if you are to buy a house, by conducting some research on the stock and going through the Jigsaw Puzzle Model. If you find that you do not understand a stock, then avoid it completely.

In investing, what everybody knows is not valuable to us, because we are more interested in companies that are not covered by the media and command the attention of fewer investors. Preferably, it is a seemingly boring business. Apple, with its range of products, such as the iPhone, iPad, and iMac, just to name a few, is most definitely not a boring business. With all due respect for the late Steve Jobs, we will stay away from this company, as it has to continuously innovate to come up with newer and better products every other year. Now take a look at a social networking site like Friendster.com. It used to be on the top, but what happened to it? It was replaced by new social networking sites, like Facebook and Twitter. So, what is next?

In investing, what everybody knows is not valuable to us because we are more interested in companies that are not covered by the media and command the attention of fewer investors. Preferably, it is a seemingly boring business.

Understandably, it is simply impossible for any company to stay on top when it is in an ultracompetitive industry. What happened to Nokia? It used to possess one of the biggest market shares in the technology industry, but they have lost out to Apple. Yet, in another industry, that of chewing gum, a company like Wrigley does not have a pressing need to upgrade their products each year. In fact, the greatest innovation is probably in the form of product packaging, whereby the management team has to decide on whether or not to change it.

Investing in high-technology companies is very common among investors today. To them, Apple Inc. might seem very attractive, in view of its popularity. In our opinion, it is better to focus on simpler, even boring, businesses that are sustainable even without having to go through any major overhaul in the next 10 to 20 years. To help you better identify such companies, you can ask yourself this simple question, "Would I continue to use these products or services if it remained unchanged in ten years?" If the answer is yes, you have found a company to invest in. Otherwise, avoid them. You can also ask yourself, "Where would the business be in the next ten or twenty years?" In this case, the vision of the business is not stated by the company, but by you, as the customer, after scuttle-butting. If you cannot see where the company is headed, it is useless for you to own its stocks even for a few months.

By and large, there are companies from other industries that can better withstand the test of time. In relation to this, we can safely say that people will still take trains or buses 20 years later. And people will probably still drink Brand's Essence of Chicken, which is produced and distributed by Cerebos Pacific Limited. This was our conclusion after we asked our friends (who know nothing about investing), "In ten years, will you want your kids to drink Brand's Essence of Chicken before an exam?" and most of them answered with a definitive *yes*. In Asia, for many decades, we consume a wide range of beverage products, including Milo, which is produced by Nestle (listed in Bursa Malaysia). We will continue to do so in 10 to 20 years. Needless to say, do your homework, such as checking its numbers, management, and valuation, before investing in any company.

On top of avoiding technology stocks, do not invest in initial public offering (IPO) stocks! You can still make a fortune on a company after it has successfully developed its products and services, and its successful formula is replicated. In our opinion, it is all right to miss the first wave. Wait until the company has been listed for at least three years and has a track record to prove its worth. One good way to monitor such companies is to get a share from the odd-lot market and attend its annual general meeting.

Mistake 4: Investing in Companies that Are Not Consistent

In a growth company, we like consistency in revenue, net profit, and cash-flow figures. Consistency is the key to an ideal growth company. Successful companies always leave a trail of success. If the company had been growing consistently in the past, there is a higher chance for it to grow consistently in the next 5 to 10 years.

Consistency is the key to an ideal growth company.

It is important for us to find a company that performs consistently, so that we can predict its future growth rate. If the company is inconsistent, investors would be unable to project the intrinsic value of the company. Now let us look at the example

Table 10.1   Earnings for Company A and Company B ($ million)

Years	Company A	Company B
2005	1.00	1.00
2006	2.00	−0.50
2007	2.50	5.00
2008	2.90	−0.20
2009	3.00	1.00

of two companies in Table 10.1—one that reports consistent earnings and the other with significant fluctuations.

Based on the information in Table 10.2, you would definitely want to invest in Company A, because it shows some predictable patterns in its earnings as compared to Company B, whose earnings experience such sharp fluctuations that you are unable to project its intrinsic value in 10 years.

Apart from ensuring consistency in revenue, net profits, and cash flow, you must also outline a table to include other key ratios, which will enable you to spot any manipulation in numbers on the part of the company. A table would make it is easier for you to study the company's trends. Companies with a three- to five-year track record will offer enough information by which to study company's' consistency.

Based on the information in Table 10.2, we can look for any improvement in the company from year to year. Here, investors need to find out the reason for the sudden drop in net profit in 2008. With further study, it can be seen that the business had an exceptional item that amounted to $0.4 million. Thus, the actual net profit should have been $1.13 million ($0.73 million + $0.4 million). Using this table, it would be much easier to spot inconsistencies. Based on the table, net and gross profit margins had shown improvement from 2005 to 2009. This was followed by an increase in cash. The amount of debts also decreased each year. Overall, the report is positive as bad numbers decreased, while good numbers grew.

For instance, although sales figures decreased, it was followed by an increase in net profits. You should then read the annual report to find out what is the main cause. For this, the explanation should be simple and logical. If not, stay away from the company as its management might be cutting costs to increase its profits

Table 10.2   Table of figures to study the trends at Widget

Year	2005	2006	2007	2008	2009
No. of Outstanding Shares (million)	23.00	23.00	23.00	23.00	23.00
Revenue ($ million)	5.00	6.50	7.10	8.40	11.30
Cost of Goods Sold ($ million)	3.90	4.80	5.00	5.80	7.00
Gross Profit ($ million)	1.10	1.70	2.10	2.60	4.30
Net Profit ($ million)	0.70	1.00	1.20	0.73*	2.30
Inventory ($ million)	0.12	0.21	0.20	0.25	0.50
Trade & Other Receivables ($ million)	1.90	2.20	2.50	3.10	4.00
Cash & Cash Equivalent ($ million)	1.00	1.30	1.50	2.00	3.90
Short- & Long-Term Borrowing ($ million)	1.00	0.60	0.30	0.00	0.00
Current Liabilities ($ million)	1.70	1.90	2.10	2.35	4.15
Shareholders' Equity ($ million)	4.00	5.30	6.20	9.50	6.70
Operation Cash Flow ($ million)	1.00	0.90	1.10	1.20	2.89
Capital Expenditure ($ million)	0.20	0.35	0.30	0.31	0.56
Free Cash Flow ($ million)	0.80	0.55	0.60	0.89	2.43
Dividend ($ million)	0.00	0.15	0.20	0.25	0.40
Gross Profit Margin (%)	22.00	26.00	29.60	31.00	38.00
Net Profit Margin (%)	14.00	15.40	17.00	8.70	20.30
ROE (%)	17.50	18.90	19.30	7.68	34.00
Cash Ratio	0.59	0.68	0.71	0.85	0.93
Debt to Equity Ratio	0.25	0.11	0.05	0.00	0.00
CAPEX Ratio (%)	28.50	35.00	25.00	42.40	19.30
Dividend Ratio (%)	0.00	15.00	16.00	34.20	17.40

*Exceptional item in 2008

temporarily, instead of increasing its net profits by selling more products.

Mistake 5: Buying a Growth Trap (Not Focusing on the Quantitative Side)

There are investors who are willing to invest without a margin of safety. Here, the main culprit in buying a stock at a premium price is greed. When investors start to see prices of a stock increase tremendously, they are likely to put more money into it in the hope of benefiting from its growth. This leads them to overpay for the stock.

A growth trap occurs when growth investors overpay for a company's stocks in the hope that it will grow further. By overpaying, the investor is subjecting him- or herself to more risks. The purpose of this book is to teach you how to minimize risks by having a minimum 50% margin of safety. If a stock's intrinsic value is $1, you should buy it at $0.50. The margin of safety is there to buffer any wrong assumptions made. In this case, if the actual intrinsic value is $0.75, you still have a margin of safety of 25%. Thus, it could reduce your risk and maximize your return further.

The key in preventing a growth trap is to never overpay for a growth company, regardless of how attractive the company is.

Another situation occurs when investors calculate the intrinsic value of the company at the start, thinking that the company is a good bargain, without understanding the company's business, management, and financial numbers. Intrinsic value should only be calculated when investors have done all their homework on the company and want to know whether the company is undervalued or overvalued. You can, of course, start with a valuation to identify bargain stocks before you carry out an analysis based on the Jigsaw Puzzle Model. This is, in fact, one of the quickest ways to hunt for good growth companies that are selling at bargain prices. However, if you have identified a quality company, based on its business and management, but find that its valuation is overpriced, you should keep that company on your radar and wait to purchase it when the price for the company falls below its intrinsic value.

The key in preventing a growth trap is to never overpay for a growth company, regardless of how attractive the company is. In which case, Q&M Dental might be very attractive to us, but we are holding ourselves back until we get a good price from Mr. Market.

Mistake 6: Buying a Value Trap (Not Focusing on the Qualitative Side)

The opposite of a growth trap is a value trap. It is the result of one of the biggest and deadliest mistakes when investors hunt for undervalued stocks and rely too much on fundamentals, in this case, being all about the numbers.

The best investment in the world is a growth company that promises steady growth and is selling at a discount to that growth rate (e.g., price-to-earnings-to-growth [PEG] ratio 0.5). It has been consistently growing at 15 percent per year, while maintaining a return on equity (ROE) at the same rate as revenue, earnings, and cash flow. However, investors should not assume this will continue at this very attractive rate. If investing was so easy, this book would be much shorter.

Financial numbers are based on the past performance of a company. While these numbers give us clues about how the management team managed money for shareholders in the past, it is definitely not a true reflection of the future. With the understanding that not every growth company is guaranteed to grow at a certain rate, it is your job to study a company based on qualitative factors (e.g., business and management) to ensure that it is able to sustain its business and continue to grow in the long run. As the company grows, its intrinsic value should grow as well.

> *Many value investors commit the mistake of focusing too much on a business's fundamentals while they ignore the management team's quality and future profitability of the business operations.*

If a stock is priced low, first and foremost, you must find out why the stock is cheap, because what is cheap can become cheaper. One common reason for bargain growth stocks is that the company might have released bad news, such as poor results or a lawsuit. This often poses a good opportunity to buy stocks that are cheap and undervalued. Next, our job is to determine whether this problem is permanent or temporary. If it is permanent, avoid this company. If it is temporary, you might have found a bargain growth stock that has not been appreciated by the market yet. For instance, Design Studio was in a lawsuit that sent its price decreasing from S\$0.60 to S\$0.45 in just one month (with its price-to-earnings ratio trading at 5.4) in May 2010. When we found the problem to be temporary, after doing all the necessary homework (e.g., scuttle butting by meeting with its management), we purchased the stock at more than a 50 percent margin of safety. Another reason for a cheap stock could be that the company enjoyed zero growth in its business, due to its inability to introduce new products or services to drive earnings.

Many value investors commit the mistake of focusing too much on a business's fundamentals while they ignore the management team's quality and future profitability of the business operations.

There is no lack of S chip companies (China-based companies listed in Singapore) that not only appear to be very attractive, based on numbers alone, but can be scooped at a great discount to their intrinsic value. However, most of them are value traps. Owing to the prevalence of management issues, such as fraud and dishonest audits, you need to place more attention on the other three pieces of the Jigsaw Puzzle Model when assessing such companies. Unless you have a certain edge in the country, you should not invest in these companies. For instance, if you are living in or have relatives living in China, then you should have an advantage over others. In this case, you have probably heard some news through scuttle-butting that has not yet been released to the public.

At this point, let us talk about an S chip company, Oriental Century. A provision of educational management services to educational institutions in China, this company was listed in June 2006. Reviewing Table 10.3, you can see that it was a very attractive company to buy, based on its quantitative factors alone.

On top of that, the company did not incur any debts. However, in March 2009, it was discovered that the amount of cash and cash equivalents reported in the balance sheet was substantially inflated; it was alleged that the CEO had made them all up, using fictitious accounting. Needless to say, those who invested in this company without ascertaining the credibility of its management suffered great losses. Here, the key lesson is not to judge a company by its numbers and valuation alone. These are hard quantitative measurements. In addition to such quantitative measurements, you have to assess a company's business and management as well—these are qualitative measurements that can be determined through scuttle-butting—to ascertain whether a stock is able to last in the long run. If all points favorably, then go ahead and buy it! Otherwise, do not invest in the company, even though it is cheap.

Table 10.3   Financial numbers of Oriental Century

Year	2004	2005	2006	2007	CAGR
Revenue (RMB million)	42.0	60.5	67.8	73.9	20.2%
Net Profit (RMB million)	23.9	32.5	33.9	38.5	17.2%
Operation Cash Flow (RMB million)	11.2	49.9	34.9	43.9	57.7%
Cash & Cash Equivalent (RMB million)	18.6	64.8	149.6	190.4	

Mistake 7: Sell Your Winners; Keep Your Losers

Most investors sell their winners the moment that they realize profits and hold their losers in the hope that the company will bounce back. This is a big mistake. Instead, we should be selling our losers, while keeping our winners!

Research has shown that winning stocks often perform better after they are sold, while the losers continue to languish. This study was done by Terrance Odean, who examined the trades of 10,000 accounts from a nationwide discount brokerage. He found that investors are likely to sell winners after a 23 percent gain in their portfolio, with one stock representing a quarter of the profits. He found that, on average, investors are 50 percent more likely to sell a winner than a loser. He also found that those winning stocks continue to beat the market by an average 2.35 percent. Also, investors are prone to letting their losses ride. Based on the study, it is obvious that investors sell winners too quickly. On the other hand, investors also like to keep losers and wait for a period of time hoping that the stocks will bounce back and then sell them. The reason for this is that investors can boast when they sell winners. On the other hand, no one wants to lose, and realizing a loss is painful. Investors try to avoid being a target of ridicule by selling a loser and realizing a loss. If you sell your winners too soon, you no longer reap the benefits of a compounding effect, while the losers will continue to eat up your profit by performing poorly.

If you continue to leave your capital in a value trap company for that same 10 years, you would end up with a loss. Do not compound your losses!

Investors should start cutting their losses when the fundamentals are deteriorating; it will only hurt the investor if he keeps holding onto the company. By doing so, let us say he loses 50 percent of the initial capital, but takes the remaining 50 percent of the capital and invests it in a fast grower (20 percent per annum). By the end of 10 years, he will have earned back his losses. But if he continued to leave his capital in a value trap company for that same 10 years, he would end up with a loss. Do not compound your losses!

Mistake 8: Diversification Mistakes

These mistakes are also often caused by greed. When a particular stock is rising in price, investors ignore the need for diversification and place all their money into a particular rising stock in the hope of garnering as much profit as they can. This, however, is a common trap: When investors place all their cash into a particular stock only because they believe it will never go down, when, in fact, it will.

Another common belief is that overdiversification significantly reduces one's exposure to risks. This is untrue. On the contrary, overdiversification leads to poor returns. The problem here is that, when investors diversify beyond more than 10 stocks in a developed country or more than 20 stocks in developing countries, it is going to be extremely difficult to monitor them. In other words, it is definitely easier to monitor $10,000 placed in three to five stocks than to invest that same amount in 50 different stocks. It will not only make your investment harder to monitor but will also subject you to commission charges, which are very high when purchased one by one. Do not overdiversify, which would actually contradict your goal of beating the market, because profits from the winners will be diluted by losing stocks.

There is no end to the kind of mistakes that an investor can make when it comes to investing. This chapter cannot cover all possible mistakes. For instance, there are some mistakes that are not reflected in your portfolio but cannot be ignored. These are considered *omission mistakes*. Another mistake would be investors being reluctant to buy a stock that has gone up in price, even though that company is still undervalued and has a good margin of safety. Such an investment mistake can be exemplified in the case of Investor A when he bought into Japan Food at S$0.26. In this instance, Investor A did all the necessary homework and concluded that Japan Food could be a potential growth company. He lined up to buy its stock when it was valued at S$0.26 and had a huge margin of safety of more than 60 percent, but failed to do so at that time, as investors were only willing to sell at S$0.265. In this case, the difference between the ask price and the bid price was $0.005! Even at S$0.265, he calculated a margin of safety of more than 60 percent and insisted on lining up for the stock when it was priced at S$0.265. Eventually, he never purchased the stock, and it surged to S$0.28 the next day of trading. Now, that was a foolish mistake, but it was not the end of the story. After failing to buy, he decided to recalculate the margin of safety when the stock was valued at the new price of S$0.28. Interestingly, the margin of safety was still beyond 50 percent! He assumed that the stock would fall back to its original price of $0.26, but, sadly, it never happened. The share price of Japan Food soared to S$0.43 within four months! That is 60 percent in capital gains (assuming he got in at S$0.265). Although the mistakes were not reflected in the portfolio, it was certainly painful for Investor A.

There is a saying, "Penny wise, pound foolish." You do not have to wait for the share price to drop. As long as there is a margin of safety of more than 50 percent, you should not hesitate to take action. The key lesson to take away from this chapter is to learn from as many mistakes as you can during your investment journey: Be it from other investor's mistakes or your own mistakes, it is best to identify them, learn from them, and not repeat them in the future.

Summary

- You are a long-term investor and think like one. Never attempt to time the market.
- Do not invest in an IPO stock until it has a three- to five-year track record.
- When assessing fundamentals, the key word is *consistency*. You could get into a growth trap if you buy a growth company at a premium price (no margin of safety).
- Check on the credibility and integrity of the management team; focusing on numbers and valuation alone will lead you to a value trap.
- In the long run, sell your losers and keep your winners.
- Keep your portfolio to fewer than 10 stocks if you intend to invest in developed countries.

CHAPTER 11

Case Studies and Conclusion

Congratulations for reading this far. In our bonus material, we showcase five companies as case studies and demonstrate how we apply the model, from the perspective of value-growth investors. Download the case studies from www.MillionaireInvestor. com/5-case-studies.

We have long heard predictions of the end of the world and continue to hear of them now. If the world is indeed coming to an end, it would seem illogical to invest in the long run. Instead, we should simply splurge and enjoy while we still can. However, none of these predictions has come true. This book was published in 2013 and, amazingly, you are still here, reading this book. Life goes on as usual.

Just as predictions about the end of the world are flawed, predictions as to the direction of the stock market can be just as flawed. All those so-called experts have made countless predictions that were just plain wrong. As we have seen, despite the onset of many natural disasters, including earthquakes and tsunamis, many new millionaires are still being born. In fact, more and more investors are becoming rich through different types of investments. It could be through real estate, equity, or a combination of both. The key lesson is not to be swayed by these so-called experts from the chance of prospering if all things work out well. Instead of mulling over things that are beyond our control, we should do the things that are within our control, such as investing as a means to protect our finances for the future.

In general, value-growth investing focuses on the qualitative and quantitative sides of a growth company., It is important for investors to understand all the hard facts that others do not know.

To sum up this book, you must understand how a value-growth investor is wired internally, by having the correct mind-set. We look for growth companies with great products or services whose management team is aligned with shareholders' interests and whose fundamentals (numbers) are strong. We will purchase them when they are undervalued and sell when they are overvalued. Ultimately, this book is designed to cater to investors during the bear market, in their bid to protect themselves against any potential capital losses. This requires the investor to understand the business inside out—including risks managed well by trusted management—thorough fundamental analysis and having a wide margin of safety.

With the use of the Jigsaw Puzzle Model, we are confident that the whole process of investing will be much easier for you, as you endeavor to ascertain the value of a company, according to the four pieces of the puzzle. By following this model, you will not miss out on any key information. And, in doing so, you will have a greater advantage when it comes to decision making. Ultimately, it is all about buying and selling at a price to someone who is willing to sell and buy, but knows less than you do. With this, you will be able to get multi-baggers in return, with growth companies that are consistently generating over 15 percent compounded annual returns.

Here, we summarize the model step by step.

Our recommendations for assessing the business are:

1. Start with a simple and boring business.
2. Invest in a company that is in line with a business that you understand or is inside your circle of competence.
3. Find out how the company can sustain itself, that is, its economic moat and competitors.
4. What are potential growth drivers in the future?
5. Understand the risks.
6. Do scuttle-butting once in a while.

Our recommendations for assessing the management are:

1. Trustworthy—act like an owner and do not take excessive remuneration.

2. Candid in reporting—own up to mistakes, if any, and address the issues.
3. Aligned with shareholders' interests—do not issue shares to dilute shareholders' interests.
4. Track record—sound knowledge and experience in the company and industry.
5. Growth plan—set a future plan to grow the business internally or through complementary acquisition where business cultures are aligned.
6. Doing scuttle-butting by attending annual general meetings.

Our recommendations for assessing the numbers are:

1. Look for key performance indicators, such as revenue, profits, and cash flow to determine growth.
2. Understand all three statements—income statement, balance sheet, and cash-flow statement.
3. Know how to calculate financial ratios and compare these with the company's competitors.

Our recommendations for assessing the valuation are:

1. Calculate all the three valuation methods—price-to-earnings ratio, price-to-earnings-to-growth ratio, and Discounted Earnings per Share model.
2. Determine whether it is undervalued, fair valued, or overvalued.
3. Protect downside risks using margin of safety.

Once you have found all the information about these four pieces, you will know when to buy and sell, according to the Jigsaw Puzzle Model. Remember, all four pieces of the puzzle must be in place before you can buy. Sell when one of the pieces falls off.

Up to now, we have covered what you need to get started on your investment journey. However, the end of this book does not mark the end of your need for investment knowledge. We encourage you to continually upgrade yourself, as this book alone will not instantly turn you into a successful value-growth investor. You have to continue learning and be willing to allocate the time necessary to sharpen your understanding. It could be learning from others' mistakes or reading any materials that focus on long-term investing.

Mistakes are inevitable in investing. However, knowing how not to repeat the same mistakes is often difficult and requires discipline.

Thus, successful value-growth investors should continuously learn from any new mistakes while eliminating the old ones. It is dangerous to blame mistakes on others. In doing so, you will never learn from your mistakes. Instead of shrinking from responsibility, own up to your mistakes and apply corrective actions to prevent them from happening again, thus making you a better value-growth investor. Take responsibility and be accountable. Continue to expand your knowledge of investing. Widen your circle of competence as you continue to acquire new knowledge. The bottom line is to have discipline, commitment, and practice. Lifelong learning is important.

Mr. Cheah, chairman and co-chief investment officer of Value Partner, changed his signature when he was 25 years old from his name to "Learn," so that he can remind himself to be humble and learn new things each day. In his opinion, commitment to learning is one of the major traits of a civilized and responsible individual, whether you are a fund manager or not. In this spirit, keep learning.

It is okay to be an old-school investor, as long as you generate consistent returns in the long run.

In addition, we have to become old school when it comes to value-growth investing since we neither follow fanciful technology stocks nor subscribe to modern financial methodologies. In our opinion, it is okay to be an old-school investor, as long as you generate consistent returns in the long run.

In the course of this book, we have tried to shed some light on some of the complicated issues in investing. You might have initially found some topics to be difficult to comprehend, but you now understand them with the use of a simple model. With this knowledge, you can make better investment decisions for yourself and quickly act upon an investment opportunity when it arises.

We would like to thank you for taking the time and effort to read this book. We will continue to pursue our dreams and live out this awesome and rewarding investing journey. On this note, we wish you all the best in your investments in growth companies. If you happen to meet us down the road, do say "hi" to us!

For any feedbacks, testimonials, or inquiries, please email to: feedback@8investment.com

To access our latest articles, visit www.MillionaireInvestor.com.

Bibliography

Buffett, Mary, and Clark, David. *Warren Buffett and the Interpretation of Financial Statements: The Search for the Company with a Durable Competitive Advantage.* London: Simon & Schuster, 2008.

Collins, Jim. *Good to Great: Why Some Companies Make the Leap . . . and Others Don't.* New York: HarperCollins, 2001.

Cunningham, Lawrence A. *The Essays of Warren Buffett: Lessons for Investors and Managers.* Singapore: John Wiley & Sons Singapore, 1997.

Fisher, Philip A. *Common Stocks and Uncommon Profits and Other Writings.* New York: John Wiley & Sons, 1996.

Graham, Benjamin. *The Intelligent Investor—Revised Edition.* New York: HarperCollins, 1973.

Ho, Kok Mun. *How to Make Money from Your Stock Investment Even in a Falling Market.* Kuala Lumpur, Malaysia: Kanyin Publications, 2007.

Kaufman, Peter D. *Poor Charlie's Almanack: The Wit and Wisdom of Charles T. Munger.* Marceline, MO: Walsworth Publishing, 2005.

Lynch, Peter. *Beating the Street.* New York: Simon & Schuster, 1993.

Lynch, Peter. *One Up on Wall Street: How to Use What You Already Know to Make Money in the Market.* New York: Simon & Schuster, 1989.

Mizrahi, Charles. *Getting Started in Value Investing.* Hoboken, NJ: John Wiley & Sons, 2008.

Montgomery, Curtis J. *Building the Perfect Portfolio.* Singapore: WallStraits.com, 2004.

Neff, John. *John Neff on Investing.* New York: John Wiley & Sons, 1999.

Schroeder, Alice. *The Snowball: Warren Buffett and the Business of Life.* New York: Bantam Dell, 2008.

About the Authors

Victor Chng and Rusmin Ang are the chief investment analysts at 8 Investment Pte. Ltd., Singapore. Together, they specialize in unearthing high-growth, small-capitalization companies. Currently, they are managing a private equity fund of over $5 million.

In the course of their work, they regularly network with CEOs and key management of public-listed companies in the region and have supported over 300 investors in teaching them how to discover undervalued, high-growth companies in the market today. Their goal now is to grow their fund to $150 million.

Index